NEW AND SELECTED POEMS

Also by J.S. Harry

The Deer Under the Skin (1971)
Hold, For a Little While, and Turn Gently (1979)
A Dandelion for Van Gogh (1985)
The Life on Water and the Life Beneath (1995)
Selected Poems (1995)
Sun Shadow, Moon Shadow (2000)
Not Finding Wittgenstein (2007)
Public Private (2013)

J.S. HARRY

NEW AND SELECTED POEMS

Compiled and introduced
by Nicolette Stasko

First published 2021
from the Writing and Society Research Centre
at Western Sydney University
by the Giramondo Publishing Company
PO Box 752
Artarmon NSW 1570 Australia
www.giramondopublishing.com

Cover and design by Jenny Grigg
Typesetting by Andrew Davies
in 9/15 pt Tiempos Regular

Printed and bound by Ligare Book Printers
Distributed in Australia by NewSouth Books

A catalogue record for this
book is available from the
National Library of Australia.

ISBN: 978-1-925818-57-4

The Giramondo Publishing Company acknowledges the support of Western Sydney University in the implementation of its book publishing program.

This project has been assisted by the Commonwealth Government through the Australia Council, its arts funding and advisory body.

i.m. J.S. Harry

1939–2015

Contents

From **A Dandelion for Van Gogh**

Introduction

Over thirty years ago I met J.S. Harry, fittingly or perhaps ironically, because of a bird. Readers familiar with her work will know that Harry's keen observations of avian life make up a large portion of her poetry. The bird was a rainbow lorikeet named Birdie – rescued as a chick after falling out of its nest. At the time, Harry was poet-in-residence at the Australian National University and needed to make up some potion for Birdie which required a food processor. So she called us as the only people she knew in Canberra. Arriving with barbecue chicken and chips as thanks (this tells you something about her as she was a lifelong vegetarian) she proceeded to mix a batch of mysterious ingredients which included bee pollen. When we moved to Sydney, Harry often visited us carrying a very large cage decorated abundantly with native flora and silver beet leaves. Birdie was left free to wander around – much to the delight of my five-year-old and the utter fascination and confusion of the dog, who couldn't take his eyes off her. She was so well cared for that a miraculous egg was eventually laid to everyone's surprise, as much as Birdie's.

During her time at the ANU, Harry was expected to meet with individual students, and conduct workshops. We attended readings, which included her fellow residents Jennifer Maiden and Vicki Viidikas. It seemed Jann and I did a lot of driving around in her huge blue-and-white car talking about poetry, becoming friends easily and quickly in spite of the vast differences between us and our work.

When she returned to Sydney we spent hours on the phone gossiping and reading our poems aloud – eventually sending copies to each other. I remember sitting in my little study in Narrabundah and opening her letter that contained one of the first rabbit poems, 'Calcutta'. I laughed out loud at the wicked satire, the ingenious originality of it. Eventually the rabbit poems were collected and published in *Not Finding Wittgenstein* by Giramondo in 2007. It won the *Age* Poetry Book of the Year Award. The eponymous rabbit hero of the series was called Peter Henry Lepus, and was said to have Creole ancestry. Originally the rabbit was based on the beloved children's books by Beatrix Potter but the request for permission to use the character was met with such outrage and the threat of lawsuits by the Potter literary estate, that it left Jann with a lifelong terror of copyright.

This was not the end of Peter Henry however. He went on to meet many more philosophers and travel to the Middle East, in poems which were written near the end of Jann's life, and are included in this collection.

Jann often met me after work when I flew to Sydney for consultancy work; one time for dinner in the rooftop restaurant of the hotel where I was staying. Ordering fish for her, thinking it was a suitable vegetarian dish, I watched her pick at it while we looked at the neon skyline of the city. She never said a word. Another time we sat on the floor of the hotel room and ate salads from David Jones (I was a bit more cluey by then), talking about poetry and reading aloud. Having sent her a new poem, I was anxious to hear what she thought. In her typically frank way she said the ending was 'flat'. As I attempted to defend the last line she asked me to read it aloud. I did and she admitted that it worked perfectly with my voice. She was inflexibly honest and yet also willing to accept that she might be wrong.

Jann was the most charitable and caring person I've known – supporting all kinds of poets and buying poetry books even though it seemed she had no money. She was also immensely private (partly the reason for the use of initials for her public name). Two male 'senior' poets showed up when Jann launched my first book, and told me that they were only there to see if J.S. Harry was a man or woman. Apparently there were bets on it. Until her health began to fail and she needed help to shop and clean, I never knew where she lived or visited her house. Her usual shopping list was mince (for the birds), white bread (for the possums), cheese slices (for herself) and stationery supplies. The house was so full of papers and books it was hard to walk around.

Jann came often to our various places in Sydney and we would talk sometimes until four in the morning – she drinking the strong black coffee I would brew, I wine, and both of us smoking with gusto. This is when questions of whether a 'holey doily' was a tautology, or whether a full stop or a colon was best, would be discussed. This may sound silly or boring but it never was. Amongst other things Jann could be very funny, with a dry Australian sense of humour. Her vast knowledge made conversation fascinating. We were both reading Wittgenstein and other theorists on language and poetics. Jann was extremely precise in her work and these apparent incidentals mattered. I think that a fundamental dichotomy in her approach caused her some existential angst: how could she make the poem as exact as possible and yet still leave 'room in each poem for the imagination of the reader to move around in'. She eventually came to an understanding that enabled her to write brilliant and satisfying poetry embracing Bertrand Russell's notion that 'a word has a meaning, more or less vague; but the meaning is only to be discovered by observing its use. The use comes first, and the meaning is distilled out of it.'

Around 2005 Jann moved to Katoomba to be with her partner and fellow-poet Kerry Leves and we didn't spend so much time together. She had known Kerry for many years – since early workshop days. It was during this time that she put together *Not Finding Wittgenstein*, no doubt with Kerry's help. Later they moved back to Sydney so Kerry could begin a PhD. But in the end he was unable to finish it. He died about six months after receiving a devastating diagnosis. As usual she let her poetry do the speaking for her: the beautiful poems that appeared in *Public Private* (published by Vagabond in 2013) express her sadness and loss but also her stoic resilience in the face of it – turning to the natural world for solace and celebration.

I remember one time when she called me to read a poem she was writing, published in that collection as 'Plop!'. Because it was an early draft (Jann wrote and printed numerous drafts – sometimes up to twenty or more until she was satisfied – all of which she kept for future reference) she was experimenting with the laugh of a kookaburra. She actually imitated the bird very well and tried out different possibilities in the poem but I still didn't think it worked. She didn't say anything else about it but when the poem appeared all of the kookaburra sounds were omitted.

By then her own health battles had begun in earnest and she spent a great deal of time in hospital undergoing surgeries and physio. Eventually it was clear none of the surgery or other cures were working. In spite of the short notice, her family were able to find a place for her in a nursing home where she could receive round the clock care. At first Jann was totally resistant to the place and very suspicious, as one would expect. Eventually she settled into a routine and even became fond of the carers her family hired to provide assistance in areas the home could not. For six months or so we (Rob Shield, a friend she had earlier met when he was called to fix her computer) worked on the Peter Lepus poems that can be found in the final 'Return to Baghdad' section of this book. They were already past draft stage and just needed a little fine-tuning. Rob mostly read them aloud as Jann didn't particularly like the way I read her work and he was most familiar with them. She had a remarkable sense of cadence and even when she was very ill, she could pick a misstep or a false line break. Corrections were made on the computer. These poems are highly detailed and fairly complex. Harry had kept a very close eye on the events unfolding in Iraq and was somewhat expert about the political situation, using all of her skills as an autodidact to consult multiple resources including a huge collection of newspapers. The poems are not as humorous as the early rabbit poems, though the unusual characters and satire relieve the seriousness. They are intensely critical of war (as she had always been as far back as Vietnam) and the stupidity and cruelty of human beings. Peter Henry Lepus has finally had his rabbit eyes fully opened and he has sadly become somewhat cynical.

At some point a *New and Selected* was mooted and we switched our energies to working on this volume. By that time Jann's illness had progressed and she was often in pain or fuzzy because of the drugs she took to ease that pain. Very quickly she decided to cut three or four poems from the selection, but from there the task became much more difficult. After spending weeks, sometimes months or years, crafting a poem it is very hard to abandon it. But space was a significant problem, as she had gone on to publish seven collections after her first, *Deer Under The Skin*, in 1971. It was all a little unorganised and we weren't getting very far so I typed a list of all her published poetry to help organise the process. And we went from there – each time a poem was read it was given a cross, a tick or question mark. Still, it was sometimes hard to stay on track, as the discussions about the individual poems went off in all directions. There were poems we didn't even get to. The list became invaluable in deciding the selection – the more ticks, the more solid the poem's place in the collection. In finalising the contents I read and re-read the poems. I could hear Jann's voice (she was always a magnetic reader) and sometimes I felt incredibly sad that she was gone and I would never hear her again. There were times I had to make an editorial decision – the responsibility weighed heavily on me but knowing Jann so well, and being privy to the discussions around the poems, I am mostly comfortable in choices that could easily be said represent the *best* of J.S. Harry.

In the last weeks of her life Jann asked me to ensure the

New and Selected Poems would be published. I promised I would make every effort to see that it was. And with the help of Ivor Indyk and Rob Shield, the book you are holding in your hands is the fulfilment of that promise.

Nicolette Stasko
Sydney 2021

The Deer Under the Skin

1971

the what o'clock

A puff-ball
on a slim green stem
is more attached
to earth than I.

The wind will tear
its seeds away –
perhaps they'll root –
Words root. My words? Mine?

Living all in your head
is a kind of thistle-madness,
anyway, but, close, grass is,
birds are –; the people
outside
          seldom sing.

People in pain
I brush against;
I rip. And they hold me.
But, when I roll away,
in my mind I am a puff-ball
about to leave earth;
again,
          the wind isn't far away.

How?
Grown from a thin green shoot
with a root in earth
to this airy death?

Even as a child,
I could feel   for days on end
the isolating air, cool and strange,
around my head

how old Pity left the poem

So then I smashed him up
systematically
bashed his face and bled him
he slid down the wall
over-ready
The blood brightened
his greasy clothing
He was making some slight sound
I must have hurt him
bad as I had to
When I bent down
to find out
if he was going to go on feeling
he said something
out of half his mouth
– I am the bugger he said
I am yourself:
Now go –
tell it like a joke

the little grenade

The little grenade
wanted poems that explodexplored
or pushed candles
inside the pumpkin people
to make flames sputter and drip
where their darkness bulged.

The he that was a friend of the little grenade
liked poems that sat fatly in the middle of stillness
                    waving their feelers
The poems the he wrote were lumpy mattresses
stuffed with kapok. Or flock. (The little grenade
wouldn't lie down and think in them – didn't lie down
and feel one – ever.) They had the kind of stillness
that goes to museums   on sunflecked Saturdays
to be glazed by the marbly stares behind glass.

The he didn't like the friends they made.

He's friend the little grenade
once had a book Hegel   who said:

                                                            'If reality is inconceivable,
                                                            then we must contrive
                                                            inconceivable concepts.'

Most of the things the he could not imagine had happened.

He read   aloud   alone:

'If reality is simple
must we contrive   simple concepts?'

It was dusk. A deer grazed the forest's edge,
moving nearer. While he was liking the gentle deer
a small neat hoof
stripped his liking like a meat fillet from his shoulders.

He didn't believe that either.
It had happened.   What then...?
and he thought
there will be room for explodexplore   and stillness
in one of the corners. He knew that

TO START WITH

Everything is a *large* box – you can't see into it,
to start with
right around it in the middle   or much of it to end
with –
He didn't *want* to put string and paper round it –

He *liked* Everything – he wanted to get into it –

He felt the bounce of a poem in his palm,
coiled himself around, and like his friend
the shattered little grenade,
he threw himself.

the outburst

The thunder is trapped in the sky above us,
like a roar in a small box.

Perhaps he is hoping by raging
as he trails the teeth of the lightning
to shatter the box which contains him
and break
                    into the open sky.

There was no box:
He smashed...he thundered against it...

to know himself
created 'closed sky' :

This too
if we make momentarygods
each of each...

to choose? to make such a noise.

ask, respond!

Ask, respond! – the voiceless flowers –
their bellmouths
ask   by being.

Softly, softly as almost
softly as silence
the sky whispers rain.

Your questionbegging feet
bruise buttergold
flowers. They tread
like milch cows
on green things.
Question, answer!   feet
press earth,
weedslime slowly seeping.

the gift

After last week's heat...
I was going to bring you
a basket of perfect,
scarlet tomatoes,
until I remembered
I had forgotten
my suit for the tournament
and that you would
probably use them
at the poetry workshop
tonight.

into the landscape

The waste from the chemical factory's stacks
shivers on the wind
in the world above the shallow drain-fed lake...

Here where delight is a paddle-and-splash,
mothers can see
that the notice-board's warning
of danger-in-bathing
is wrong.

On the dark wet bodies
a mosaic of grits
surprises the eye
with its violet and brown.

Coming in from the sea,
the sand looks beige,
and the lake-outlet merely a dribble.

It has all been accepted
by the fifty fairy penguins
dead at the lick of the tide.

'Dead. Died. Will Die.' – Oh no –

A fox is dancing on the hand of a man
in a cafe at the Cross.

His arm fits through its belly.

It is strange to see the deathless pet
leaping across plastic tables.

Twenty glistening firemen
who have come to see the fire
brush past the fox; in their brass helmets
the are larger than people; they
do not see the fox, and the
fire is not there.

The fox snaps air and strains towards space.
The man in the fox dreams of chickens.

Even when the man turns his laughing-mask away
the fox quivers like a habit.

Foxlegs droop when the man's legs walk;
when the fox moves, people are joyful.

When the fox dances
people's faces are so joyful
the fox may live for ever.

in the park beside the marina

Gently, insistently, all day
the voice of the rain.

It spoke beneath the baked skin,
under the public tufts;
it seeped beneath the roots
of scurf-dead surface grasses.

Softly it spoke,
through the earth, to the seeds…
hard cases
swelled, transmuted.

Some bodies
are closed to the rain.
Frangipanis, face-up,
accept all of it.

To breathe, to drink –
with the rain,
to be grass…

The spinster-owners
of the icecreamshop
feel, with the rain,
their losses.

parts towards a meaning

1

The gift…a day…light, sun, shadow   in all of it.

Men are putting sewers into the history under victoria street
beside each hole, two piles, separate colours, chalk and flesh.

If it were egypt they might be digging for pictures –
links with the four thousand year old dead
                                                            Outside a delicatesser
a man in a white coat scours the pavement   the dust waits   cree
under feet   to ambush him from the floor.

                                                            Even the number cod

on a sydney county council substation
means   inside the ring of its makers   the meaning equal to the
     use   as it says
in a birthbook of myth and language –

I sit in a bus   focused behind my eyes. A thin, bone terrace hou
inscribed 'poet and peasant'   says it has rooms to let –
they are all inside –
Upstairs an old man peers out through shroud-muslin,
between the iron bars I peer through, looking in…
he would like goats
his trousers…cast like dice on a bush   once   they ate them
real goats … outside his head …

2

give him proof   he cannot feel the bus ticket under his hand
he is afraid   that the trees and people will be taken… :
that they were never real

3

In a summer park, young leaves are greenness like dancing.
My nose is a bee on the rim of the vat.
If it could dance, turn and circle how far to the honey,
if the swarm would leave the hive…
Eyes press against the edges of things – sometimes they penetrate –
soft   inside a colour – like a flower…
the earth is held together by the roots of strong grass called bilin
during earthquake   I have to work to find nails…
the purpose of grass is the purpose of nails is the purpose of words…
I have to work to feel shaped sharpness grip like grass…

wiremesh baskets proffer packaged stiffness for the
mummification of heads
chemists sell it   there is no need to go to a chemist I will give
it to you
Soul Pattinson's baskets hold stuff-to-preserve the hair the
face the feet
where
is the formaldehyde for the feelings   bottled dead   inside
the selves?

under trees the shadows go back like pansies black black deep
    into the sun
here under the white needles of the hoses everything is dripping
onto
/
downfrom
/
grass
b
l
a
d
e
s
:   the wrists, the ankles know

gross, red-toed pigeons walk to bread
at the hand of a two-foot boychild in red sandals

...and somewhere   for the third time   a swimmer goes down
  not really perturbed
  if the cramp in his gut is like envy...

4

Perhaps there is a rite for the days that are not felt
a ceremony for the harvest
                    of the intangibles...

Primitives believe nature
yields nothing
                                        in return for merely human labour

tell me a name   that its power may come through me
Language, a field...?
                                        if you can work it ...
The Nile came   at the word of Ra
                                                    to irrigate the dry of Egypt

Perhaps there is a magic
                                    the knees angled
                                                            what angle appropriate

and to whom?
                    (and the serpent coiled in the curve of the rain
                      will it ever   swallow the child to spit forth a one
                        strong with the old wonder...)

5

death on a page   crickets in winter
the hang of it is loose   the way of a tree on a summer evening
who   sane   would be like a word
                                                of which only one use is recorded,

that, heard at a distance
                                    by a man with half-use of his ears...

leaves, trees,   live in their uses   Egyptians
caught on tombs   in the ancient glyphs
by scarabs...

6

...alive   through the mouth of a cobra...

who created all things   yet not this one ...
when it bit, he was an old god who dribbled
when it bit, his spirit cried out like a child
his body was Egypt
lit petrol
ran through his veins

a quibble – the snake not his...
kneaded from the dust where he spat
by Isis
his granddaughter...

Who...
promised to take the fire,
if he would tell her...
Ra god of the mountain god of the morning
Khepera at dawn Ra at noon Tmu in the evening
it is written: Ra gave Isis eye of the moon,
eye of the sun,   that the powers
pleased her
(the secret name is not transcribed – its power

was transmitted in silence.)
Ra took up
The boat of immortality, became
its helmsman   steering the dead
across skies of winestain
and lapis lazuli...

a shard or a piece of the hull will not do...
I have grown four thousand years old
looking

old man I could not make you a goat
the snake I made is a liar
...alive through the mouth of a cobra...
To be believed
do not come
unless you are shaped as a
question

a question that strikes
four thousand years back
is not your answer
...under shadow...
where belief...

under trees
belief of pigeons
turns to bread
at the hand of a two-foot child...

one, in the motel

One, in the motel,
bleeds, and cannot be stopped.
Endlessly, the flow
saps, reduces the span.
Across the highway
hessian-coloured sheep
drift, halt,   drift and eat.
neon-green paddocks' long-grassed spring
augurs well for summer.

It is the Abattoir's paddock.
The sheep put down their heads and eat.

words and mouthings
the personal assertion

everybody is trying to sell it –
not just
    politicians
    students,
    preachers,
    people circumlocuting at the wayside chapel,
    homebodies
    thesis-writers
    taxidrivers,
    foreigners and secret drinkers –
    even that non-commercial
    odd-ball the poet –
    even the blind-deaf-mute –
    wearing out, on the platform at central,
    spuming at the mouth, writing
    incomprehensible
    syllables with his finger –
name a person – he's pouring it –
    gurgling it
    scratching it
    screeching it
words – words the push.
    ears aren't thirsty any more –
    ears are shut – and don't want any
    part of it. the mouth, now, that's
    what everybody has –
    open for business.

behind death

even from the tombstone they thrust:
'*i* worked, *i* lived, *i* died, *i*'
to the ear, the ear, the ear on a living head –
no wonder van gogh –
when colour was his sound
and people
kept trying to mess it up
falling into his ear
too often
in the wrong colour – he was not
mistaken for a public receptacle
after he took it off.
there should
be a less-red way
of taking the sign down
so as to stop
all these misdirected people
endlessly following a sign an ear
endlessly mumbling and muttering
all the long way back
from behind the sign
to where the system is blocked off.

the ossuary of dreams

There is nothing to say...
Silence...A great gloved hand
reached out in the night, and
loosed its cats upon the land,
to smoothe a silence on those streets.
Power in the trainer's palm – claws sheathed in the grab of night,
those trained cats froze in a stalking squat...
While darkness prowled across the land,
night black-bandaged the eyes of the children
sleeping, dreaming of...
        sweet speech, words on paper; – toys promised...
Prague radio's closing anthem-strains
twanged night's false tune to the wakeful.
Morning woke tank-grey, curling its vaporous mists
over the faces of the hopeful.
The invading sun shot streaks of red,
a new breed of riflebirds crackled and spat...
On the cold morning of a plot-black night
menace purred that the dream was over.
But some stepped on to the unmade track
of the strange beast's tread, and will not move;
Meat...meat...The bones of dreams
re-flesh from such rich treasure.

to a writer of epitaph-epigrams

your verses are smoother than honey
consistently
there are no
        raw brown sugary grits
left clinging sweetly
to stick and dissolve,
in the cracks between the teeth.

Turned out of a buttered pan
words boiled uniform like honey-toffee
harden remotely,
set   sweetrock on a sheet.

If there were bubblings and hissings,
shrieks from the time they sailed-living
canvas flapping, loose ropes trailing,
you,
      did not give them a wind.

Becalmed on the pages, caught in their own Sargassos,
your wordships' hulls are grown upon by weed:

children least of all   would visit this place
to find the men
           who sailed to die here.

(Few of them
can be taken these days
by a lick of a buttered sweet).

Pointillist landscape

White flowers,
on the waves of green morning:

the wind on the fields
comes in from the sea.

Apple-blossom
illumines
the cottage-garden.

The sun spills –
Itself!
Follow.

To a world
where the wind
calls the fieldflowers to move
  – through light –
to the time of the flowers on the sea.

Kaguya-hime

Adapted from the Taketori-Monogatari

One day a farmer cut a piece of cane –
The bamboo, split, contained a tiny girl,
a perfect doll, three inches high; he took
her home. Her eyes shone clear as star-points when
he named her his own daughter: 'Shining Girl':
her face grew fairer than his own; of all
she was most fine. When she grew up, the rivers ran
wild with the tales of this flower's unfolding,
and far beyond the farthest snows, eyes burned, and suitors
came, to seek her love. Their eager faces in her head
swam many as small silver minnows, swimming-
drawn-to-seethe in one small space of sea.
To each she gave a task; they were not easy,
as he who did the thing she bid would win
her love and she was only one. The cherry
blossoms came, and fell, and seasons fell as petals
from the trees – and far apart, like fishermen the suitors spread,
each tried to net the wish she had decreed.
At last the sky reclaimed her, in a chariot
of joy – she winged her way beyond their arms
in the season when the cherries drop their leaves.

waiting for the express, to go north to Ôsaka

At the station
they said it would be three hours.

People
did not come.
They knew.

Soft white flakes
sat
on your sleeve.

We were afraid
to go away.

You did not
touch my hand
in the new style
but
the snow
melted on your eyes.

Those three hours sat as lightly
on our hearts
as the snow upon your sleeve.

to Shiki who died of consumption

'The hototogisu
is said to vomit blood and die
after it has sung eight thousand and eight times' –

I do not know
how many times you sang,
growing thin over haiku and waka,
growing thin...
From your bed
through the window
you looked into the autumn;
upon the screen the shadows
of the dragonflies grew thin.

(White the papers on your desk
the sudden stormwind...):

opening your cool throat so clearly ...
then burning, 'how deep is the snow...'
'how deep is the snow...'
you sing, hototogisu, you sing –

it looks nice and quiet down there

We are the unworthy –
carrying a load of love;
it weighs us to our knees;
we cry and pray, we are not fit
oh lord, give us knee-strengthening games
that we may be ready,
prepare us to stand upright, our women on our backs,
exerting pound for pound pressure,
upward.
On second thoughts, lord, if there's no time for that,
send us a pneumatic-tyred sound-proof cart;
at least if we are to be crushed,
our screaming needn't be heard
and you can carry off our disjointed remains
        quietly.
In some other training centre we may learn,
through discipline and muscle-building exercise,
how to push back
exerting an equal pressure
on this most powerful love.

the deer under the skin

Standing at the top of the hill
pricked by the wind/ pricking to it
the sun shooting weirdly/ flashes of silver
the light through the clouds/ like a glare off ice

With the clouds/ herded-heavy/
grey-white/ wind-harried/ running before it/
flat as a dog

Trying to take in the light/
to clasp the wind and grasp hold/

Skin...the pine-patterned plain/ dark green
miles of it/
goldlakes of cleared-land
the sneaking pines circling upon it

Somewhere there – deer too / feeling this wind
standing breathing listening hearing...
no sound/ brown   pine-needle-soft /
nothing but the wind   the green shushu...
                                        sudden/ the whack
of a rotten-limb's drop / the startling
bell-magpie   startled at last.../

Having run with the deer always...
pine-shielded on a path apart/ ...when startled

the fences were often   too tall to leap to Escape
...sometimes to get there...

Lately the deer   have been too short
for the top barbs of all the fences
            palpitating gently
            they run   turn   stand   and are smashed
Soft-dead   they flow to the guns

the twentieth century playing a kind of barmecide with its poets

I offer you food, many bowls of it –
You lift a bowl, to sup and smile
and smile to taste, most strange
and subtle flavours. Lifting each bowl
you comment, wryly as in
ancient Baghdad, on the wondrous-shaped containers
the exquisite light of glazes.
Your appetite is endless.
The richest game, the choicest fruit
our tongues may touch
I offer you.
Each empty dish your mendicant hands
accept and savour.

yellow without poetry

canary   a piercing pipe of yellow sound
lemons tinkling on a tree like ice
sunflower   seed-headed   vein-knotty pregnant
gold   soft dead   a shape of death
bananas ripen jungle shadows warm as the place where the tiger la
papery buttercup, thinner than a grass stalk
frangipani cream goes into butter, tactile
                                                                butter
            feeling round in itself...

      yellow knife spring   and lemon winter sunlight
              reflections of sun off Australia Square
                    mock
            a martyr in a businessshirt

yellow is a cockatoo: crested alarm –
yellow, a sound like a bellbird:
        a bellbird makes a sound like sunlight
        down the darktunnel of a treefern valley
        to a smell of deadfern

        yellow is the trumpet of the prostitute's old hair

        a tongue of sunlight on a ridge of tired snow

        yellow is saying I am warm:
        yellow is saying this is winter; feel the death,
        under my deceiving skin

yellow is what the palewhite faces of the clouds
          would be
                    if the sun came out

yellow is a sound that is not afraid of itself

yellow is an unready apricot
trapped in a bottle where mould's begun

yellow, a fullmoon   on still black water,
pulling you down along its shine

yellow is jaundice
deadpeople's babyclothes
moth-delighting wedding gowns,
small, sieved smiles

yellow is the beach in the bottom of your shoe,
spilling on the floor, in the bathroom,
shining   shining

yellow is fluffy like dogwattle   fat balls of pollen
people afraid   the sound of sneezing
to break a bough   to take indoors

unpeeling: a paddling song

everyone is waiting for something unknown/
to blow them over/ tonight
known things like water trees square sheets of tin
blow suddenly strange in the wind
everything is hair
black/ wiggling through water

each drop on her big as the world round and tear-shape
they cling clear and shining/ they sit unattached on the
night is by Blackman
white teeth dark water dark road/ bare like body-ghost
legs under raincoat/ whose legs whose stocking who's unpeeling
who is who someone's stripping you the dead one clammy nylon
        from her leg
white feet exploding and the mind fused dark/   out out
dark feet dark waters dark
soul you are here in the
rain your breasts are pink to the

you did not come the wind's a reflection misting across
white lights blow down the rain arrows straight to the heart of the
bare flesh bare legs shoes you were always a shield against feeling
bare and the whips of the rain score the old skin like deathknives
the wind is a scream this is death/ someone's splashing/
I waited for you to come tonight

somewhere tropical

Even the monkeys in the public gardens
are divided into tribes and have partitioned
the fruits and trees of the lawn on which we sit,
into their various and particular tribal grounds.
Watch them even now as they play;
                                        should one
                                                        stray
across an imaginary frontier,
a seething biting troop
of border guards
descends, to drive him
back, across the invisible parallel,

and yet, how quiet they seem
before and after
when feeding from our hands.

honesty-stones

The land between us
had grown so bare
the landscape so denuded –
all we had left was what we knew –
just the rocks and the shade they cast –
your eyes my eyes, across them.

We did not need to speak, to talk.
Everything was in the rocks.
It had been said before.

We could not live there

coming and going: peripatetic poet

It is not
          that what you see
when travelling around the world
is significantly different
from the land you are leaving,
rather, that what you observe, returning,
although seeming the same as when you left
in itself,
is viewed altogether differently.

Having realised you cannot depict the world
in which you are travelling –
its guns, nails and cash-registers
turning you blindly back into yourself –
you realise, now,
shut in your own state,
you cannot see that, clearly.

To make the agony of the condition
real, you must accept
the full weight of the pressure out –
the torn flesh, the cries, the hostilities;
in order to return,
with a traveller's eyes,
to the miserable hearth you left.

watching a blind whittler under a redwood born 82 years before christ and thinking about a tree in disney-land

a dream grows in disney-land,
sixty feet high –
prime quality plastic
durable brown and green:
a psychologist nailed its slats
up the trunk to the crotch
where the children
                    writhe and scream.

everyone's dream
                    turns back on itself
one hand on its peanuts
                         in huckleberry's tree-house.

no need for renewal   the foliage
cleans well   and is
comfortably ample.
a dry wind blows:
the vintage-children
clamber, ecstatically shaded by plastic,
blissfully
released
from the unreal.

almost classical – autumn/ winter/ winter/ spring

1

For late autumn
a warm wind.
On the back fence
chrysanthemums
hang exhausted.
Flies are few.

The day dawdles
the flight of the butterfly
the sound of the flying boat...

The kitten curls its tongue.

2

No carpet – the floor at your flat.
Sitting on it.
Waiting for the kitten
to die of cat-enteritis?
Dosing it – vet said
it may recover.
Four of its brothers
did not –

3

the floor
is cold
... scouring:
the kitten
insists not to feel it
... gripping...
she draws blood
through the skin of your blue leg.

4

Spring – not quite –
the wind still sharp.

The kitten waits by the door
to start.

The young shrubs you planted last summer
are gobbling the blue through the window.

Re-discovering the rathole she grew to
squeeze through, in the autumn,
the kitten goes out.

showing ourselves to the neighbours' children, Warragamba

The lions about to receive –
cross-pawed in the shade,
or strolling on the road
among the Holdens.
An inbuilt tawny sovereignty makes
the park-rule, 'lion-of-way',
quite meaningless:
they do not recognise
we have yielded and are prey to half a fear...
(the glass/ is glass, there's no one near,
a lion's paw...)
We are *almost* as the apple-mouthed pigs
served in hotels on platters at Christmas:
how clever we are, how real –
you could say we look alive –
you could say we were asleep.

To serve animals with animals whole or only
slightly dissected – is natural –
a front leg, hoofed and hairy,
a maned, unskinned, Cyclop-eyed,
perfectly split half horse's head...
A little blue tractor darts up
on high mud-caked tyres,
to drive them from the road.
It is feeding time – we start to leave –
they do not hunt, they do not kill –
shambling quietly to their tea.

the catcher

Being unable to dance, being unable to sing –
what else could I do but catch them falling?
    Some fell like bubbles, like thistledown, laughing –
    and some fell like people weighed down by themselves –
    every day every hour the shapes keep on falling...
    squatting, sitting, weeping, floating
    being – something – to themselves, new ones
    settling, fleshing bone-breaks –
    animals land softly thudding,
    bats like moth-cries, birds like feelings...
    sometimes cars fall; owners with them
    metal-shiny slip through air...
Mostly they changed when I touched them.
And I cannot juggle with the order –
    my empty hands leap and twitch and cry
    and it seems that they are full.

boat for a voyage

It is always moored
in the middle of the harbour...
Nobody is seen on board it.

Sail-boats, speed-boats, row-boats, cruisers,
other boats...
have the clouds and the sea in their paint,
hulls of smoke or snow or sky,
masts of fleece or polished wood.
They all tether near the foreshore
round the buoys.

IT
broods, in the middle of the bay,
its stem and stern pointing upward...
its tiny cabin lacquered dragon-red.
The death-black hull, from stem to stern,
wears a ribbon of dragon's blood.
The three red masts are never rigged.

As its crew drift out and waft aboard,
the boat goes out without a sound –
at any hour of any day.

letting things work variously   towards definition

loud   through blackness
the feet of the roaches
crackling the empty biscuit papers
at the bottoms of boxes
at the backs of cupboards
lust dry as taffeta wrinkling crumbed greaseproof-
wrappings of the mind's old layered bread –

know them   by touching   if you can without writhing
the skins of old loft-apples where they move
like silent hairs

glimpse them   at midday   scrambling darkly round the boiler
hidden   heated   hating
daygrey winter-air
clearly   themselves   yet fiercely
evasive, blind-
ed by techniques of
electric glare –

independent   (defined-at-night
by a torch-eye   focused obliquely)
curiosity quiver-legged   whiskered
intensities,
burnished queerly-
shiny like greed

glistening over dark surfaces feeling everything
with the feet –

hard-backed scattering; scuttling cracking loudly:
dangerously loud for Illusion's feet –

sometimes things at the backs of cupboards
rustle louder with the lights off

sometimes
roaches can be caught
by the intellect pulling a switch

Hold, for a little while, and turn gently

1979

Hold, for a little while, and turn gently

He conceived of a style that would stick us to its idea
like a dagger;
he conceived of the idea (that the ideal style
would join us to)
as part of our body (which
in literal fact it was   or would have been)
since, as he said, only the written spoken or otherwise
manifested idea   can be said
to have an external 'behaviour'
and we   were very   silent.

He conceived of a style that could
rise up   off its page
and stop us cold as the steelpoint
sunk in, upto its hilt,
yet making fire
in the belly.
He did not say
that the man with the
dagger in him knows pain. He did not say
that a man   is unable to test
the 'fire' of the pen
pinned to a wall through his belly
by stiletto. He did not say
that the stabbed man
is the symbol of fire, he did not say
that the man is   the animate
animalburning

What he did say was
that the Cora Indians   do not find it meaningful
            to distinguish
between the words of a man and his deeds   between
the sounds of a 'mind'   and the moves of a body.
When we had proved, to our satisfaction,
that he was not   a Cora Indian, (and that there was,
            for him, some slight nuance
between the sound of the idea-knife in his
  'mind'   and the feel of a blade in his body)
            he was quite dead   and the distinction
meaningless. It was then
  we realised he had intended
            for us to test
his idea, like this, on him,
from the beginning.
            Hold, for a little while, and turn gently
the word-knife in your belly.

What might pass a man as a survivor

I see you   lizard
whitebait with legs
pulse in your side
pounding like an
apoplectic head
like I could be a threat to your
biologic survival
like you haven't
weathered millions of years
by just such   evasive stillness
grey posed on splinterwood
only the pulse pumping
what might pass   in a man   as fear...
what might pass   a man   as a survivor...
                and when you move
                                the sun spears your side
like it strikes the sides of smallfish
arrowed in the shallows   a watery shiver
they turn and dive
                        quick silver lizard
under the hydrangea   leaves the colour of old spent blood
past the tomato plants grown scraggy with the cold
under   thin lost bums of fowls left without feather
over the sun's weed beaten winter yellow
over dry white sand black specked like whitebait eyes
past where a fungus mounts   feasting on tomato stems
suddenly – lizards everywhere –

loudmarch on dead autumn
live   over dead leaves go
retreating
lizard feet.

In a Goose-Month

The way spiders
spread their gossamers
between the eyes and the moon
floating for miles
out across black

To web, the world,
this twig, that fence,
starts here – and the eyes
take hold imagining
gossamers stretch – from star to star –
Distort, of the eyes as a
black, night's frame, against which
spinnings
take
their chance –

Spiders, webbing, stars, spinning
all
out
of anyone's grasp

Used to be
the month they ate
the goose, more
gossamers veiled

the gardens'
mists and grass

Small, not-seen

spiders spin
Gossamer is, does

It will stick
most anything
between your eyes –
a horse, a house
a door
way's hole, binding
it gently
down to ground

Else, floating loose
on a wind your breath
light as touch
which the wind
cannot hold – still,
which the wind's
touch sends –

under the rim

under the rim, 4000 feet,
going down
towards ranger valley lying low
lost blue as a myth of bushrangers
between green
hard-to-ride-over hills,
a kangaroo went up the
nearest slope, to brush,
away
from us

he stopt
on a rock
posed side on, halfway up,
large, his tail
-fur outlined black –
rich brown   inside the black –
looking back

at the ute   to see
what we
were   what had
become of us
objects   there
at the feeding
hour   amid cattle
stopt   towards him   looking up

below
on the valley floor
above last night's

rainfresh green grass, late
mountain summer's yellow daisyflowers,
green and yellow grasshoppers
rose upwards   by wing
flowers moving dreamlike
from their stalks

This Cool

This cool
near-dark
holds nothing:
it is over
a wide stretch
of the Mann
River; four
barely visible
threads
slant
towards unseen catfish.
Barbs grab weed:
near bottom.
Nothing to smell except
rain   as the rain
moves down
from the mountain
sound rippling
the surface, the near
green leaves;
the river –
in flood –
dark   mudsilver.
Ten sky-pinned swans
stroke silently
up stream.

Across the river
on a high, dark hill
a bull is roaring
          to another
paddocks away.
One
of the lines
goes taut –
by the kerosene
lantern
          's light –
landing
          a one-foot eel;
in the gully   above
rain has moved down
on the unsurprised
black noses
of two wallaby.

Tell Me What You See Vanishing

Tell me what you see vanishing and I will tell you who you are…
W. S. Merwin

1

I went to the place of two years back:
that shell was under the sea.
Only a mailbox
stood above the tideswirl.
I choked on its singular cry like a gull,
but swallowed
                its angular pour
of the letters written by fish.

2

Now we have come   to gut & scales, & turned
with a killing-intent, to the shoals, to prey,
perhaps we will find our letters…

Those people from whom the letters
do not come   must be somewhere within our reach…
unless they are behind, fishing us, on the last tide
in the place towards which   we can never
swim   or fishing the ocean, outside the reef,
or in some hole we have forgotten, which formerly,
we used to dive, for them…

If it is true we never wrote
                                        to them or they to us
without sign we have exchanged ourselves endlessly.

Somewhere on an unvarnished hull with the paint
peeling from our eyes like skin,
we are waiting for them to grow tails, to rise...
for ourselves, to sin...for continents
to begin...
The lost continents continue. Whales like dead armies sing.

the hill

it is strange to speak
of the hill as 'rising'
when the hill
stays exactly
as it always has

like a blue background
through a woodhut window
on somebody else's act

it
isn't going anywhere
as a person
might
get up out of an armchair

from under the lapful
of vegetables – peeled –
to find some food for a cat

presently it will seem
to the ones who are climbing the hill
though they say – there – it rises –
that it is they

who are doing that
bush flies rising with them
cling to the shirts' wet backs

the men climbing are too engrossed to look
at the view they are climbing above

eyes close on a problem of finding footholds
they sieve with their eyes and hands
the firm rocks from the loose

beneath them   way down in the valley
through a bush hut's kitchen window

someone with a telescope is looking up
not seeing
the hill at all – in the blurry
worry – of watching – counting
the small figures rising

counting them   counting them back

'the baby, with the bath-water, thrown out'

: it will not seem
a meaningful exercise, to them,
to hunt new life
to stuff this particular cliché

the small foetus
already on its way

through the grid
at the bottom of the shower-alcove

even here needing help
under water pressure
resistant
to being broken up

They will not meet again

Each pair of eyes
reminds the other
of an eyelessness

that joins them

Dropped also by accident words
do not fall with
an unborn's colour

Nor
do they need to be pushed

in quite the same way
to be allowed to fit

through a grating –
The shower-pipe leads straight to the main drain
which is mercifully silent
                                        no acknowledgement
appropriate, for so small
a sac of blood

One of them will stay on
in the apartment

above it –
pale chook on a china egg
set to brood for a century

a quality of loss

‘fire’ they cried in the middle of the dance,
wheyfaced girls and weary men came pouting out
their faces rekindled by a vivid life
because it was a fire: a need – somebody’s house
was burning up.
                                        It could have seemed that what he had
was burning in that house. It could have seemed he saw his days
on fire, and the leafless trees
stood away like fishbones in the dark.
His chairs were on the coals where the flames died
and the smoke trailed out
                                uncertain as a dog.
And ‘fire’ the dancers cried, again, as a latecoming wave
                                surged out;
they held him back
when he tried to go inside
the burning doorway of his golden house;
late   one had asked, and he hadn’t remembered,
what it was, of his life, that he’d lost
that he could
have brought out, if he’d had the time –
from the glowing bones of the liquid fire –
                                                He’d long remember
something else   how a dog might try
to re-take a haunch   had and buried   years before –
vague, a trace, the dimmest scent –

Late he circled
round the black down-dropping struts,
held, by their stares, as perfectly
as a bee, by a glass   around a flower.

Backward Over Dark Water

The trees & the flowers cast deep shadows
Tree-lilac makes blue breath
Who will pick up
this scent
            & give it
                        to the ducks that've
brushed their undersides
on the muddy edge of the lake
cried once   just there

& gone for ever...

On a manmade wooden bridge
a small boy with his line
wound round a cork & his hook
jagging a bright
mortal grasshopper

is fishing He says he has seen
a golden fish in another pond yesterday
It is that golden fish he is after

His hook is too large
for the mouths that are dreaming in water
       here...for the mouths of the pond's
live monsters...

The grasshopper will die soon
It will lose   clear sap   It will drown
among duckfood   Already the underside
of the pond may be gathering
an insect's darkness

The words do not pulse – fat & gold – in his hand
that would tell how an uncaught fish   may last

how an uncaught fish may gleam...

without having flipped out of its life
behind a curtain like the dusk
in any
time gone backward
                              While the boy
holds a hand
to a line of dream
uncaught fishes will follow him always

they say

they say   a worm under cowturd
yields the black pig delight

all night i have been fighting, for an image,
of black roots, & thick-white grubs & bulbs
caught in a tussle of night & dark

the white bulb wants   to push up   through earth
to the fresh wet airy light
it is angry

to make a flower

the black root's dream
is of earth and death   it would lock
like a ring or a promise
forever   going down

somewhere above a black pig
is rooting in the dark
the raw green herbage, in the
wombat's steaming shit
where the trawling midges

hang a living's clouds

the ancient dead send rosearms
out of a headland

beyond eyes' mirror   it is filled
with planted people   they
storm the air like flowers
they smell too sweet for health
                                        a planted
people   blackening   in air   above the ground

the rose thorn cane & leaf
search air
the taproot eyeless blunders down

Outposts

Taking a shell he had never seen
for a boat
he began to paddle.

He could gaze, over his shoulder,
to recognise
through which waves in the word 'came'
he had passed.

Countries he landed on. Islands he clove in two.
The appearance of phenomena amazed him.

When the lakes he fished for Jungian archetypes
turned to mudholes yabbies were friendly.

Mountains he avoided. The sea though familiar
was never monotonous.

'Lost' he realised last, as he looked around him,
as the chalk weeds and bird-derelicted landscape:
it was a territory to which no rescuer in the world
carried maps. No one in the world
would be sent to save him. And perhaps,
here, there would be time
to make a journey.

It was then he began to search,
slowly at first, for the signposts. Night
had become a constant. Though there were stars
they were painted on his skin – no guide
to navigation for a revenant.

Only emptiness to fill his way? His ways had fitted emptiness
as the sand makes a place for a shoulder, as the sand
takes shape, round a body, without coercion.

Emptiness was all his ways had mapped with truthfulness.
In bayou-marsh he'd traversed by a fantasy of stars,
once luck had gone, he found no substitute
for the paths he'd not recorded. When he came, at cost,
to the seas he'd left, he found his shell was smaller,
the ocean shrank beneath his touch, and quaked, away from him,
as if it were human.
Going away from himself in the places that he'd been,
he was moving ceaselessly   over ocean.

When the air stank of rotted vegetables, two days before he sighte
the land it came from, he knew the voyage would end soon: that
would have to.

Even a distant outpost has its two-headed calves and its curios.
He put himself quietly ashore on the landing.

And saw that the trees held fruit, the harbour fish.

It could have been the place he started from.
Nobody could tell him for certain. Nobody alive remembered,
and he himself was not sure, that this was his place.

It could be as good a place as any. There were words for sale
in papers. Daily consulting
Situations Wanted, he found no reference
to himself. Wanted, he found no reference
to himself. Found Columns failed to find his ending.
It was as if he and the voyage had never existed: they would save
no lives, make no discoveries. For the first time
in over a thousand dawns,
there were people
to acknowledge his redundancy.

To the courteous natives, he sold bits of string
he'd used to catch stray fishes, on the long ocean voyage,

so that people could go and fish for themselves
much as they had   with their own bits of string
in the thousand odd days it had taken him
to find their islands.

The poem films itself

Down the slimy rope   into the impossible!
The insides heave   somehow they got the camera down inside
                    the alimentary tract
The poem as a historical drama or epic
by shakespeare or a drunken lamington by somebody french who
    names
our memories 'd glided over (elision   marked by ampersand:
    digestion omitted)
will be filmed in prose our new technique (perfect
    for moribund structuralism)   The costumes
will appear to be modern, say crudely

*early*modem   ashbery or o'hara (we will not know either of
    them well enough   to differentiate)
with a few loops of pointlessly-picked-over intestine   (It would
    be 'hard'
to establish   a particular crow was here)
Though our techniques are the shirts we are betting
our horses' lives on, their bloodlines (techniques', shirts', horses')
    like those of the   abused, & fictive, 'crow',
'derive'   from the ancients & cannot be said to be authentically
'ours'   yet still the pace carries us, into the
future with a marvellous momentum We are like

the élan about to drive a gothic cathedral
upward   into havens of print /sky-high!/   happy?   heavenly?
    (exit arsehole as might be

expected'   the mixed
naturalism, & the absurd, trade-marking   the content local,
        a few flashes of unparrotlike
environmental realism, yet to be added, for the risk...

Notwithstanding
                        dead animals rising on our tongues (soap, soup,
the leather we've been chewing, round the holes
                        in our spirits' feet where the thaw, as a
melting joke leaves gangrene green as agony)
what sincerely gets to us is   :   a kind of food-poisoning

: that we are   still here   as if saving cents for a 3rd row seat
                         where
we don't want to sit   & are   already...too close up...
        from a
3rd row seat, the soundtrack-roar
                        's quite deafening...
                        (& peering)   : the screen immense in front of us
(Mute Nausea   saving up   to pay
to be itself & dead?) while from the backrow stalls we do
                        not have the bread for, they say   you can almost
see, & hear, from there...
it could be little boy blue or hamlet   who was the one...
                        by the needs of the drama managed...
to get   the shiv dug in   himself: right
                        place &
job well-done...the real, irrelevant bagpipes wailing
                        frail but true, outside (us liking them – but better:)
next role will play us into death

Between the Sand Dunes and the Cattle

Going
in the direction
of the bending grass-stalks
between the whitesand patches – windblown, driftspread
wide and smooth
across the bones of thirstless cattle
old and soft as ancient wood,

you may walk
across the path
of the one-inch
long red ant
where it   forages
translucent
amber-red as if the light
had climbed behind
the bodyjuices   inside the skin –

two hundred million years   of insect
behind its travelling – It is going
in the direction of the wind that bends away
from the ocean spray tossed upward, over dunes.

Five hundred yards inland
small green blowflies fire themselves like buckshot
from the body of the cow we stumble on.
The legless maggots have no distinct head.

Vertebrates in the live stage
being somewhat less   than useful
they do not notice us at all.

A sound or a scent starts the
dull sudden thudding:
the two kangaroos that startle
into noon.

Late a golden whistler
moves across the stillness
putting sound-pegs on his holding.
There are wildflowers on the hills.
Coffee velvet wildflowers
come one hundred times each century.
Roots pin the dustdry twiggy shrubs
to the boneholds between these dunes.

After
the sun has dropped
its compass point –
how far   there'll be no telling
north south east or west   of here or there's
the dark   we'll walk as now
stumbling, over roots and into branches.
In the spaces of the sky, five hundred years
or now
our eyes hunt stars.

A Dandelion for Van Gogh

1985

A word has a meaning, more or less vague; but the meaning is only to be discovered by observing its use; the use comes first, and the meaning is distilled out of it.

Bertrand Russell

Parts Of Speech As Parts Of a Country

1. I As Desert

I am the one of whom it would've been said –
if I hadn't done what I did –
I sit in the middle of a green land
like a consent   to its institutions. I left mine
sitting at home
like an odour of wet tweeds dogs and the British.

I came beating my stone head
against the walls of my own construction.
They were the only buildings standing in that desert.

I found when I pushed, having smashed
  through, my bloody-but
uncrackable head   emerging the other side –
having crossed   against my crushable
instincts for self-preservation –
the someone who was waiting the other side
had his axe gripped
just right for the down-stroke. If I hadn't
feared he was there, I'd never 've come –
forcing myself
                        through the wall, its alive
crustations of habit – grimy with disbelief, banging
my little tin drums and wooden scoops
        against walls' irreversible blackness –

planting one flag – here – for truth – and one –
            for the darker justice
before the axe

                    descended.
                                        (The order
I founded
known as the Headless.) Often I am to be found
sitting in the mirage of a green land at twilight.
Like a consenting
to its institutions I am in your memory.

temple-viewing

respectfully
barefoot
mute as lovers
a pair of spotted turtle doves
enter the green silence

walking on round
brown wooden stones
sunk between
white pebbles

it is the japanese garden
to a japanese temple
the dwarf bamboos
sway in the wind
dipping
                to the soft
chimes
              of the windbells

& the doves
who are visitors
from india

nod & bow
at the ground as if
they were in accord

with both the customs
of the place
& matters invisible

Hunting dragons with fire tongues and deep smoking throats

You track for days
on the smell of one   Crossing the spoor   becoming...
Ecstasy
needs no gear   While you are hunting
and the dragon is wild-
ly twisting through jungles
it could kill you anytime   but doesn't
You follow
dropping the prints of your
progress
Your turds smoke
When
you're close
to the fire of breath
already
you are enclosing...
the equipment   not dragonshape...
the dragon...   moving...
The tighter the cage   the hotter the breath
of the feelings you get
for the dragon/
If you manage
to mesh right round   you've caught
feelings of yours which once wouldn't follow
cold thrashings of an ideological dragon/
real tail-lashings   nor even a large
meat-eating lizard   The feelings you've made

are all snarling in the cage you've made for them

They are *your* feelings

now they cannot move after the dragon

After the long hunt

they are hungry You have given them

no choice...Such a fixed place...Although curling back

their lips they appear to grow...

affectionate...

Ants follow

to the bone

Walking, When the Lake of the Air is Blue with Spring

A dark chocolate fungus
soft as the nose of a deer
nestles
into the soft,
moss-hollow,
between two
forest pine-trees

A pair:
yellow-winged honeyeaters turn
their black and white striped
bellies earthward
as they curve   into flame flowers;
one gives a gentle
come-on-now
peck at the other,
then, as if held
by invisible string
they fly fast
out of the overhead tree,
over two hundred yards
of unchosen flame trees,
into another

Out on the lake
one solitary pelican:
when the pelican

flaps his wings
his reflection
flaps back at him

Humanflung bread pellets
flip in an arc
up into air
down into water

The seagull diving
into the lake for bread
breaks into his own
white reflection

Little black waterbirds
are diving out on the lake
vanishing into ripple
their necks rise thin as snakes

A crowcoloured dog
gallops over the hill
while the voice of his colour
caws above him

Jacana

Words
in ancient times
set the halcyon-
bird –
in the calm
of the winter-solstice –
nesting
on the water of old stories

While
needs of man
walked many myths   out
over the water
birds like Jacanas
did
in ancient times build
on water
floating
factual on their nests

on the great
waterways of the world – even
on the Nile's
                    lily-pads

Had man been born
in the form

of a comb-crested Jacana
Christ
          could've walked
on the water   toes
spread out   to distribute weight
without miracle
but different – 20cm long
from bill   to tail
legs   11cm – above feet
each with a span of 15
cm – which   if they didn't
overlap
w'ld cover an area   of 170cm
                    To be
constructed
in this way   & also
to carry its eggs
under its wings   when the water
level rises   & it 's nested
on plants in – & its nest floats on –
that water table – moving its eggs
to a higher place   & to do
this same thing with its fledglings
when the monsoon fills the swamps
against it –
coupled with 1 more   adduced statistic
that its toes   7.5cm
are roughly a *third* as long
as the rest of its body
make this bird   miracle in its own

lagoon
wading or lily-walking
Seeing Jacana
is recognition
of basic
man-Jacana-difference: they do
call it the Christbird

If
the eggs
fall off
the nest
which – when Jacana
steps on it – sinks slightly under water –
they float

& Jacana can pick them up
put back – these eggs are undamaged –

Going away from you
in fright
Jacana's comb
turns yellow –
& its eggs are a miracle
of crossed reed-stalks
& purple stems
written on the shell in camouflage

Coming towards you
if you are

invisible   as reed
or papyrus
                    grass –
upon which no
bird ever wrote –
Jacana's comb is red
its back is blackish brown
its neck is yellow
& its belly white –
it is   a sight
poised   on a limegreen leaf
which sinks
leaving only
legs of Jacana
stepping
over the water

frame

soft as chamois
paperbarks' white torsos
rise out of water

like sleepers caught
in a dream by degas

there is no wind music
and they do not dance

on their
white arms
black streaks are cormorants
the brown
soft splotches ducks

ears paint
what they cannot see
in the varied shapes of frogs

rain crickets and cicadas
play the movement on

a wet cormorant
stretching to dry
is a dancer's
old black sock

briefly hung
on the air above a
bough
paint blurs line
as the sock wrinkles down

the ripples of the carp
throw rings that glide   on a water-stage
slow silent at
a particular stand
of paperbarks   there is no approbation

the willows trail
their green hair
into the blackened stage
and do not talk   though they are inside
                                the carp's language

the moon is in its first third
low   off centre
lighting the way
mute misty of face

to fade
stand
and move out

This explains...

The difference
between a chimney & a ferry
is that one   carries an insubstantial 'substance'
in a vertical direction   without moving upward
& the other   carries solids
in a horizontal direction   by its own movement

When a ferry moves the people on it
are 'funnelled horizontally' through space   to a point
that may be measured with a piece of string
& found   to be a measurable distance
from the place the ferry-with-the-people-on-it
started from

A ferry *may* move in a straight line
& return   with its solid load
to its place of origin   or point of departure

If the people on it have not gotten off
they could be described as stupid   There are other ways
they could be described
We will not go
into the other ways they could be described   nor into the act
of defining stupid   at this point lest such an enquiry
prove prejudicial to the deification of the present
& to this body's future function

The movement of a ferry is restricted
to the area of the water it travels on

The movement of smoke in a chimney
must begin at the smoke's place of origin
& proceed   in an upward direction; unless
the chimney is blocked, the smoke will seem
to escape   by disappearing   into sky   Sky

is composed of air   which may be variously described
fat thin thick hot or coloured   A tall chimney
may appear to escape   by manufacturing cloud
to cover its upper limits   However
if it is a finite chimney   it may be measured
by a piece of string   if you have a long-enough piece...
        If you do
succeed...it will be found
that the chimney has dimensions   & therefore cannot
be said to have 'escaped'   by vaporisation
into another element   What you do not know
is how the chimney   will change   after you
have finished   measuring it

A ferry may not escape in a
horizontal direction into the substance
beyond its element
without cheating exploding or changing form

If a ferry is moved by an *unknown* force, this
counts as a cheat, likewise if an

empty dragon were to bite a chimney & side-suck
the smoke, for his own, personal use,
this would be movement of smoke in a
horizontal direction, unnatural, & outside

the scope of this enquiry

A ferry may escape in a downward vertical or
slanted downward direction
This occurs if it gets sick or the guide-wires break

A ferry on guide-wires is, & moves
in a very fixed position

Smoke in a non-blocked chimney with updraughts
is restricted, to a simple upward movement
which pleases...aesthetically...by conforming   to an idea
of the movement of smoke
...idea...slowly hardening...It will no longer
be necessary   for you   to observe
the movement of smoke directly

A chimney must not move about
Chimneys on portable
houses,ships,trains, & ferries,
are excepted from this statement   see   item 21 para. 4

If a chimney carrying a weightless bodiless substance
upward
is placed on a ferry carrying weighted bodied objects

in a horizontal direction
it will become obvious   that the weightless substance
moving upward   & the weighted objects
moving sideways   are travelling in different directions
This explains   why people & smoke never meet

You say   this explanation   does not fit   your problem's
appetite...
If *only*   you had told us sooner –
instead of hazing us   with that query, about
chimneys, ferries, & *cargoes* – what you needed to know
we could have projected
an entirely different   set of developments, specifically
designed to locate
'ideally suitable stocks'
of consenting human heads
& compounds of water, carbon dioxide, sulphur, nitrogen

& even whole particles of soot or fly-ash

where they may be taken, as it were, with the one breath

Should you agree
to a further deployment, of your vital resource:
smoke: we can begin...

see item 21 para. 28 under 'self-destruct'
The Acts of the Mind as a Fascist State

Here are our heads

the gulf of bothnia

in the gulf of bothnia near the top the
salinity 's between
four to six parts   per thousand
flounder & pike   live
in the same 'sea'
also seaweed & freshwater plants sit
side by side
as grandmother & grandfather
on the verandah
in their rockers   might have done
could they've lived
in the gulf of bothnia
near the top
the land is rising at one hundred millimetres
per metre per hundred years – out of the sea –
boat houses sit in cow paddocks
falling green on their knees into grass
waiting for the sea to come back
& the boats to visit –
much as grandfather & grandmother
might've waited   for 'life' to come back
to visit them
on the old-age farm – had they lived
by the gulf of bothnia near the top –
& reindeer step down the bogs
delicately
lowering   one after the other

soft
reindeer's mouths
into the rich bog plants

cows drink the sea   in the gulf of bothnia
                near the top
fresher   water on the surface
salt-er   lower down

we are unable   to breathe
in the gulf of bothnia

though have often dreamed

of visiting   our imaginary relatives
the seaweeds & the freshwater plants

beside those ancient farms

Perisher Valley for Zbigniew Herbert

whatever we see   is coloured by the eyes
we see with   some like Zbigniew Herbert look
back at the world as if
they had lake-eyes
but the lake is blind it takes
its colours from the world

good to have something to look back on
blue as Blue Lake
on a high blue
mountain-summer day
under white cloud   or calm as a doe-eyed
vegetarian bitch
gazing gently down
on unknown   life-eating fires
as summer like a cloud

moves white
down the side of our faces' verandah
& out the valley – which valley –
                                        Perisher –'s
Spencers Creek
the eponym – James Spencer   must've looked out
over

when he was walking settlers' table cattle
from Waste Point up this mountain
for the summer pasture –

he – & his doppel-gangers – over the late
century's years – drought 1890 to
1901 – they used   to burn the mountain off
for the re-growth – then – it was allowed –

as the Aboriginals – burnt – they sometimes
must've – the mountain –
accidentally – building smoke-stunning fires to feast –
4000 years their
fossil-remnants here –
                    upon the
bogong moths

that journey all the ways but mind's
up the mountain
in grey & white barkcoloured clouds
to find somewhere mildwarm
to stay till autumn
then facing the winds
of the journey down

they came up to the mountain to rest   the moths
soft fluttering wings
being cooked off
in the fires

losing a lover/ discovering a place to keep seagoats

obverse of 'bay'
is a curve of open 'land'
with 'water'
coming into it

perhaps the convicts
used to gather rushes
on the land side
though this may
have been a dream

this tree
& the ones next to it
're white
gloved soft
in doeskin
smelling faintly sweet
faintly dry
& tasting
slightly salty
as if
the breeze from the bay
has often visited
to lick

the little seagoats
rattle their metal bells

& thrust at the sky
as if to break their tethers
if it were corfu & you were blind
you would think
you were hearing donkeys
lonely looking for owners

the gentle bitch who comes to
your hand
is black as the pitch
under trees she is lost in
though if sight came on
she could be
brown
rust or brindle
looking for a voice to put
the dance back in her walking
& the 'pitch' could be a hard strip
for 'bone-breaking' summer ball games
or the dark
intensity of crickets

the full moon
a perfect corncob gold
rises over the house of the
crocodile lady
dead prawns
ooze
out of the hands of

somebody else's lover
the fisherman

the little goats' eyes
twinkle over the water

it is years
since the sun slipped out

it is months
since you started walking

Parts Of Speech As Parts Of A Country

2. He/ He tried

He is a one of whom it would've been said –
if he hadn't done what he did –
he sat in the middle of a green land
like a consent   to its institutions. He left his
sitting at home
like an odour of wet tweeds bogs and the English.

He came beating his stone head
against the walls tradition
had built for the roles of the sexes.

He found when he pushed, having smashed
    through, his bloody-but
uncrackable head   emerging the other side,
having crossed   against his crushable
instincts for self-preservation –
the someone who was waiting the other side
had her axe gripped
just right for the down-stroke. If he hadn't
feared she was there, he 'd never 've come –
forcing himself
                    through the wall, its alive
crustations of habit – grimy with disbelief, banging
his little tin drums and woody advice
      against walls   of irreversible blackness –

planting one flag – there – for her rights – and one –
            for the darker instinct –
before the axe

                    descended.
                                        (The order
he founded
known as the Headless.) Often he is to be found
sitting in the mirage of a green land at twilight.
Like a consenting
to its institutions he is in her memory.

a shot of war

while those disintegrated by exocet
are unable to be present,
mrs thatcher – well wrapped
against the 'killing' chill
by a several foot
thickness of photographers
& 'fortified'
by the champagne-bubble-knowledge
that the war
was 'justified' – politically –
by being a success – in general –
with the british public –
& – in particular –
had improved
her popularity,
in january 1983
visits the falkland islands,
lays wreaths   on the ground
            above
'the british war-loss' –
& 'plays'
at being the one
to 'fire'
a military gun

a salon hair-do 's blown to pieces
by the force of the falkland gales

which earlier, pushed up those seas
through which, on which, & under which
particular, british, & argentinian,
soldiers, sailors & de-planed airmen
were struggling, freezing, & dying,
& she 'jumps' like an ordinary
first-time-soldier
pushed back   by the noise
& power of the gun

'kittenish'
behaviour drops from her
at this sound   so 'like'
a shot of war

underground the
recovered, drowned, burned, shot,
blown up, or frozen
are unable to oblige
by 'doing it again'
for the publicity picture

Working In The Clichés Of The 'Apple'

If you roll Pierre around
he won't grow bald spots
on his penis
I always eat a cat at 8 o'clock
When it rains I take a paraplegic
There is no savour
to eating skylarks
on the Staten Island Ferry   This
slogan 's untestable if you lack skylarks
or keep getting your
plastic palate-replacement
torn out by muggers   As a slogan
it will not help
your client's business
unless he has
(a) a more romantic site for a diner
than the Staten Island Ferry   and
(b) your other client's Italian
bottled skylarks on his menu

The image of a right whale
'll introduce 'a touch of class'
to that trip up the East River
to shoot an ad.
for a perfume which uses no ambergris

The right whale
adds a touch of class
to the 'wrong' side
of any harbour

The right (whale-less) perfume
using synthetic ambergris
will add a touch of George Segal
to Glenda Jackson's
(save-the-whale) (conservationist's?)
side of the harbour   etcetera

Sometimes when she did odd bits of work
for the advertising agency,
they let her take it away with her
like 'home'-work; she did it
riding round New York on the subway,
which was, during the day,
a home
No 'fragile addicts'
tried to stick knives into her, for money –
it was biro-and-scrap-pad work, and she
looked as she was: moneyless
The addicts had their own troubles;
sticking to their seats while their bodies
shook them to pieces
was hard enough, was an obvious...

The number of times particular kinds
of commercials appeared

in a sample of 50 magazines –
including porn – they'd provided –
was one of the things she had to 'survey',
and tote – while riding subway;
nights she took the magazines –
all 50 of them – by bus
to see the lights of Philadelphia
returning, with them, in the morning;
while everybody in the agency agreed
it made not a koala's
small shitball of difference
how this count was done,
they were happy to pay   somebody outside
                              (*and Australian*)
the client's money
to do the irrelevant work
before the faking

When all the 'facts'
were fed into the computer,
at a fee more inflated than an
about-to-burst toadfish,
they would stuff the client with
the names of likely magazines
in which to flog

a 'difficult' (though original)
who-gets-it? video game
in which little blood-coloured balls
were shot   through a maze of veins

the deadends and through-paths of which
were constantly changing
The 'target' section of the population
they were hoping to latch on to
to market this game
were those disaffiliated from   the JOYS
of HUMANITY/ the game was possibly
going to be called   how to
have A.I.D.S. and use it to remove your countrymen

It seemed unlikely
A.I.D.S. sufferers – or humanists –
'd need to buy it

Being, they claimed, a warm
Jewish agency that liked to 'do' 'creative' 'things'
'on the cheap', they were paying her –
on top of all transit costs –
12 dollars a day, out of the petty cash,
because she was (a) broke and
(b) unlikely to squeal
being without
social security number or work permit

There were side-benefits
they said: she was welcome
to take – for free –
samples of a failing-sales-
through-saturated-market
product, which a client

had given them in the late
hope they might devise
a 'new' market for it –
a video – HUNT E.T. TO DEATH – game
which initially
they had thought would go well
promoted amongst the K.G.B. as an
example of Western decadence –
for the K.G.B. to use –
to disillusion the West-attracted
teenagers-in-Russia – E.T. being a
sympathy-figure   they assumed
transcended language –
but ran into problems with the idea –
they knew no ad. agencies
in Moscow
to work with (Their sole paid contact
with the Soviets, a Russian working
in the Soviet complex on the East River,
had advised them
the K.G.B.
would be 'murder'
to extract payment from)

After 6 weeks of being too cold
and empty to sleep more than a consecutive
hour at any time – before hunger woke her –
she was grateful to be riding around
on the subway running away
with pay, for what

with or without her,
was likely to be one of the most scabby jobs
a customer could get – for a product –
in the whole
shabby city...Core? Maggots, peel and fruit/
Correction/
from 'shabby'/ The Metropolitan Museum of Art and
the Guggenheim/
excepted

tunnel vision

SUPPORT SYD VICIOUS
CUT A SLUT

JESUS SAVES   AT THE WALES

WHO ARE YOU IF YOU'RE NOT?

CREAMINESS CONTROLS YOU
OR YOU CONTROL THE CREAMINESS

screaming without words
she runs through the tunnel
straight at them
shock   opening like flowers
on the faces of the oncoming
motorists
her purple dress is ripped
to the waist so it has
become skirt only
her bare round creamy breasts
assault the pity
& the rapist
behind the many
masks of 'motorist'
her face is contorted in
the scream   everything
in her life is concentrated
behind it

she is either stoned out of her mind
just raped
so hopeless in her life
that whatever happens
will be better
drivers make
stories up
to fit some fiction
to the picture

it is 12 o'clock noon   tube
white fluorescent
inside the road tunnel
she is running on
into the citybound traffic
cars part noiselessly
around her   the traffic
streams into the city &
her bare feet & bare
breasts & scream
continue outwards towards
rushcutters bay & later
on to rose
bay if she makes it

drivers leaving the tunnel
blink at the sunlight
her image is off
their eyes   but she is running
inside them as they enter

the city
all day they wonder
did somebody
rape her? again?
did she find
shelter?

her feet were busted
by the road – they were
bleeding
did some christ-of-the-tunnel
get   out of his car
& kiss & wash her feet? *risking*
causing a chain
of deaths
to do so?

she is gone...going home
through the tunnel
drivers see
SUPPORT SYD VICIOUS CUT A SLUT'S
become 'feminised':
SUPPORT C.S.R ROT
SYD VICIOUS WITH SUGAR

& JESUS FUCKS AT THE WALES
WHO ARE YOU IF YOU'RE NOT
MY GREAT AUNT FANNY

a female
        form
                its flesh & rags
in fragments
                sea-sucked
purple
                is fished
out of the
                gap-
wash by the calm
voice of-the-evening-news
                a fortnight later

Report, From The Outlands, Mating Habits There Being In A State Of Flux

1

They've learnt to humanise
machines & build
                    their people
out of used, car-parts – the spares;
their car 's 'an almost friendly beast'. They bolt
their people's quick-flat hearts
still to a frame of mechanised lies.'

2

'At 11.40 a.m. two cars nibbling
one another's chromery
backed off, revved up,

& advanced in mating synchromesh
to twist & gnash
                  through
one another's metal moustaches

exposing their engines, to full frontal nudity:
it happened in the zeekon bros car park
at the roof level
                  on bondi

junction open
to the sky

The drivers   a young 15 stone woman   her moulding
encased in a sky-patterned tent   & the other
a 7½ stone ant woman in a fertility-print
of nuts & bolted down workers
got out & began
to berate, then punch
one another on their   design no. 9, soft as 'loo-tissue
(relic, 1980's)
faces
drawing perfect plastic blood that beaded like wine

If a little late model child who was not   lying back
on a prospect of crushed bottles on the back seat had not
begun to cry – due
to the inclusion of some – low-cost – noise additive –
which   lent him a hard-edge
isolation, from the
earlier, muted proto-types – the two cars would've
gone on – without their drivers – through the
4th, 5th, & 6th gears respectively, to meet
on the same   space (shared – like an aphrodisiac)
somewhere at bondi junction out
over the sky'

3

&   since a 'little late model child...was *not*...
lying back' etc...like a flawed hypothesis...
perhaps the two cars   *did*   go on
                                   into fusion   leaving you
where the hot-meld drew you   airborn with telescope
                                   somewhere
over sky?

Alternately, rate all premises false, drop out
            before the ending
'Two cars were observed uncoupling   at the 8th floor level;
they were going down rapidly'   If
this account of almost sighted mating

found you panting where it found us braking/

you may have been (a) a professional hot-breather at
                                                  after sex acts between road vehicles
                                            (b) about to have a 'heart' attack   Try not
to have breathed so noisily   Cars when making it

even from pervs with telescope (s)   (unable to prise
the soft   ego's bodies   out of their   defensive metals
hence braking/ 'you were   not 'safe'   to hold   this report')

                                                              like dancing hares
move sometimes   beyond the fields of the eye

Though we have searched the outlands   from end to end
...going   from dump to dump   rummaging through all
their old love comics   we have not found a single one
        where one of their humanoid engines   loved another...
& it wasn't that engine's ego that caused...

This poem ends by a pile of cooling scrap

wind painting

lake birds in wind
ride a bucking
saddle of water

afghan dogs
float in the wind
their tresses laid back
like the hair of the willow

they are dancing under

the wind's water

like a film of themselves-
in-slow-motion

the wind buckets
the lake's surface

slops tilt
over the brim

the coots
ride it out on the slant
sliding & riding
in the sunblack light
which pinks the skin

of the pelican's
beak membrane round
the lump
of the frog he is swallowing
– there – in the lee by the willow –
hawk makes the high hill
over the tossing pine trees
spire of his hunting site
& the redbrowed finches & little birds
evanesce in the short grass
blown on screams of panic
thin as grass seeds

entering the invisible

there is one fat gold
dandelion for van gogh
tethered by its own sap
in the black damp shade
by the clump of horseshit

Incident: Language, Her Form as City

The habitual
association
of a word
in a language

with other particular
words in sentences;

the collocability
say
of 'night'
with 'dark';
as when
he went
walking the
language's
pavement:

nights: the

always

moonless lightless
walking

his mind: the

language's habits

stuck there   stinking
under his foot

time in a pelican's wing

lake george's
pelicans

stationary
as elders or royal relations

immobilised
by an absence of light

stand formal

like knives & forks
stuck upright
in mud for the night

day will have them up
using themselves
differently

spooning mud
water vegetables
& fish

so what

if they've been having
the flavours of the
lakes they fished in changed

as the nameless
brands of water

were formed & disappeared

on this continent

for 30 or 40 million years

they have followed water
scooping fish frogs crabs to live
to here –

today lake george
        is the clearest of soups –

unknowing

as the tide's pollutants move
    on the shore-crabs
as the effluent flows
    down the rivers & creeks
as the agricultural chemicals
    wash   off the land
into streams

what time is left
in the flight of their wings –

unlike humans or sun
they are not
big drinkers of lakes

they will dribble back the water
keep the fish

we are joined to them by ignorance
what time is left in anyone's drink

mrs mothers day

i am mrs mothers day
i will hire myself out to you
for the 364 other days
i will not be satisfacted by
1 plus 364
grottybunches of whitechrysanthemum
you choose to offer me snottynose
i will not be placated by
a dinner a picnic
a free ride to the cemetary under yr
dog's blanket to look at a chunk of
white stone & think of yr father
yr father was not
cut stone with a jamjar
stuffed with dying flowers he pissed
on alive flowers more than once said
it was good for them

i will be yr mother
yr motherinlaw
pregnant   lover aunt sister & stranger
doing the splits like a millipede
each foot in a different cliché
yr fantasy of me wife immortally
impregnated by you: sons for ever!
i will even be yr fantasy of
how it feels

to be me sucked by you one minute
you're at my tit then it 's yr child's turn
old i mix yr faces up

i will wear my sex like
great figure with no clothes on it
i will wear my sex like a massive ladywrestler's
figure that you would like to imagine covered
i will wear you like a
loved codpiece with added
imaginative advantages
i will be yr nosewiper yr shelter yr stomach
flatterer racing tipster & bible
on all of the 364 other days
you will not believe my racing tips
till the horses win
i will defend you
against fear of yr impotence
that my competence fosters

for it will neuter us i will be strong
in the war you are in
against yr own obsolescence
for it is my war too

i will cherish you like a glass
of milk soothes yr gut & a greasy hamburger
hits yr ulcer

i will take equal money for my work to the money
you get

give or take a few allowances for sex's
unique variations
i cannot feasibly hire myself out
as a sperm donor

                    i will be yr psyche's strength
in the war of yr nerve against the steel man

you are seeing yourself as less than

& unman you by over-fuck after   if i am lucky
collecting some child that is wanted

i will pay for you to have sewing lessons to fix
up the holes in yr sox
pump up yr ego & save

every damaged dog cat chicken lizard tadpole
spider duckling you ever
give me to save   from its death   for yr temporary interest
that i will have to feed and look after for ever

as yr kodak i will not let a thing you think
shames you but i am proud of
slap to the back of the memory-bureau & lie
with its face down matting with the dust of Forgotten
i will preserve the piece of toffee
you made for me in 4th. grade inside the
indian headdress you rejected when you were 10
– which headdress you now
wish to give to yr own son   minus toffee –

i will listen to you till yr
voice runs out like bathwater

as yr wife i will never let anyone come between
you & yr mother who is not me

aren't you too stuck on the outskirts
of the day you have set me in
like a cement foot-print outside the theatre?

can we pay
              for us to come inside
                                          & play like it is

                     for the rest of the year?

do you really want   to stick neon lights in my cunt
& worship there   for the 364   other days?

now it 's
           yr turn   (off stage)   sotto nervous
who   do you want   me to be   what do you *think* to say
now that I've gone?

sleepers in a park, centennial...

overhead
scattered flocks
of white cockatoos
arriving
in little groups
're settling
their wings & screeches
in the paperbarks
for the night

ants
drop out
of the branches'
white arms
still biting
as they go
on a gravity-slippery-dip
down your neck
to the vulnerable flesh

some
late-abroad white ducks swim
on the lake
from which
their reflections
've vanished –

the v's of their swimming ripples
're broken by rising carp

half an hour
since the sun withdrew
like an 1880s
geriatric lady
dragging
its orange
& rose-robin hem
slowly
out of the black drowning water

runners' feet trip
over scentless, shitcoloured ducks
still standing, in their own time-warp,
motionless, on the bank,
though it is time
for others of their kind
to be already perching
on the arms of trees
that go swimming in water
way out   into the lake,
safe from the mouths
of hell's dogs, for the night

a solitary
yellow-winged honeyeater
calls from the tips of a banksia
where it is just too late & dark

for a human's
eyes to hunt insects

the air is warm with the scent
of joggers; putrid pond
overwhelms
early wattles' sweet frail gift

close a rat
sings to itself – high
little squeaks of exultation –
as it comes down a palm tree
for a nightly forage
round the garbage-cans
the pickings
're good   here
for a rat –
less so
for the quieter
old humans
who go through
the same garbage –
later, when it is darker –

earlier   a white cockatoo
took water
from the cityman's high-up
drinking-fountain
rather than venture
on foot

alone in the open
down to the edge of the manmade
parkes' ministry lake

the ghost of henry parkes
is still moving around
here – east Sydney –
centennial park – looking for
a 'national' monument
that didn't get built – a sort
of non-communist stalin's tomb
that was
to house –
as well as letters
art & documents –
the dead
'great'
leaders of the state

poor   as he was
for much of his life
he is wearing

his best
1880's clothes

all the birds
're welcome
here in the twilight
flying by instinct

in crumpled abandon
flinging themselves
after midges
on a blue-black sky
not one
hunts the same
crooked flight-path

Sleeping in forest...swimming in air

First up!
the early morning light

has turned day's tap on   higher up –

pale blue
spills round a
morning star –

from branch to branch

through which
light drips –

from all the cracks
and crevices of space

rise up
the sunken insects –

To angle and slant
on the waves of light?

Groundlow
the waterflow 's
pure birdcall

The Life on Water and the Life Beneath

1995

No poems can live or please that are written by drinkers of water.

Horace

The Life on Water and the Life Beneath

1

From a book of facts (he was carrying with him): *A man*
can be said to be insane while still retaining
some sanity. There is no omni-valid first point,
like a marker of no retreat, beyond which
a victim must first pass
in order to be seen to be mad. Many acts masquerading
as acts of insanity
have reasons behind them. Murder
is not a proof
                    of madness,
though it may be a sign of it. There is no
proved connection between musical creativity
and insanity. (or, to put it another way,
an indication
that you are not going to be some shit-genius composer
doesn't mean that you aren't going to grow up
to be a lunatic.)

Ten years since they'd slapped the dam
across the arse-end of the valley.

He was rowing over that lake now, above,
in an imprecise way, the houses
he and others had grown up in.

He thought of the houses as bodies
of human habitation. He wondered
how they were rotting.

Round his neck, as he rowed, over the lake above
the ground he and others had grown both taller and broader on,
across new water, Debussy – coming out of the
ear-pieces of the transistor. The
(factual chop, wrapped in a nice paper-doiley)
gentility, of the radio-station's music announcer,
the woody pears, solid green, absolutely juiceless,
of his words' contents,
clashing
against the precise,
otherworldliness of the music:

In this piece, you hear the waves
break, ripple, then build
their tide to crash again
on the spires of the
drowned cathedral.
(Clarté! clarté!
Play the piece again, to get it sharper.
Don't leave any of the
spiky – (each stands by itself
but reverberates) notes out of it.)

How   to create   a music (like it)
(as original as it was)   ever?
Debussy.

Who'd won   the *Prix de Rome* at twenty-two.
And went on from it.

2

To remove vagueness is to outline the penumbra of a shadow.
The line is there after we have drawn it and not before.
Wittgenstein

When they'd finished
the dam to drown the valley, it had been summer.
Water gathered slowly, swelling   first   inside the river.
                                        Once
the banks had been breached, there was no point
at which anyone could toss
an apple core and say, *Splash!*
That's the river. From splash-ripples out
the drowned valley starts. A vagueness
grew in people's minds. How could
any memory hold the line
of a water's silver
that had been already thickened
by the expansion of its own colour…No one
in his class had drawn it, the river, as it was.
No faithful, following, line of gums
played 'dog' to the river's 'drover'.
Gums
          were about,
                              some near

the river
            some not.

And, grey in winter, green in summer,
tippling constantly,
no convenient
line of drinker-willows
knelt, stumbled, leaned,
stood, or fell,
against their bar
that was the river.

The ford
had a pebble bottom.
Kids plashed there, after small
wet-eyed, leaf-bronze frogs,
as slim as pocket rubbers
and as droppable,
and after stone collections, that slipped
and clinked, against one another
in your pockets.

The water-brilliance of the stones
that you took home
faded into dullness
before you could show a
mother father sister or a
brother.

Where is the music for the spread
of water's silence
over landscape. What is the sound
that will silk over your ears' skin
like the silence of water?

3

It seemed, to the children watching that summer,
that the water rose almost as slowly, up
from the floor of the valley, as the bald grey hills
above the valley were said by teachers
to be shrinking. If I live ten thousand years
then the erosion of the hills
'll be as plain to me
as a Street's icecream running down in the sun,
he'd once thought, licking one's
rounded top to a point, then watching it deliquesce
as he rode back, one-handed, from the
general store, on his bicycle.
When you poured
water on rock – you got river-sound. When you
rubbed two pieces of rock together to mimic
weathering, the sound was scrape and scratching
like a mechanical rabbit trying to dig up from under dirt.
Where   was the music for erosion...
The time of the rock experiments was when
water first crept
round the grey, lichened feet

of the river paddock's
hand-axed fence-posts.

Ibis moved in as if to test
the wisdom of the insects
in their new habitat.

Grasshoppers
had water, to gauge, to leap over. If one
missed a tussock-island,
it landed clumsily in water. All legs up and struggling
it was dinner, for a white
or straw-necked ibis.

For months the paddock magpies gurgled
in gums they could not
visit earth beneath, for worms.
Feeding patterns altered.
                                        Temporarily
those magpies fed
in space;
              it was miles
to other trees that drew from peckable ground.

School   was moved
from the riverflat   to the lower hills
to squat with the hares in the upland grass
above the valley's
final drowning. Easy
to move a one-room demountable.

When the magpies moved
it was their absence
                                        rather than
their act of moving out
that was noticed.   Absence audible
as a rubber band stretched tight
that your ears
anticipate
the snapping or pinging of.

But the magpies did not
come back
to break the strand of the silence
with their warbles.

4

Worms drowned all over the valley
in the silver-clay water, as it rose.
They too   rose   (pale as the face of Debussy
in the music encyclopaedia)
bloated when their air-holes flooded.

Fence posts
became roosts for waterfowl.
You could travel along
the line of a fence
trailing an oar; there were ants
colonizing the tops

of the fence posts and when
the water swallowed the fences,
where
would the ants go…

where was the music for them…how
was it…how was it…to be transcribed?

Swallows pausing briefly
had only the top
rusty strands to sit on
and no answers.

He had seen ants trapped
on an arm of a drowned-man-tree,
its one arm uplifted save me above the flooding,
but caught, bound dead in mediation
between earth, water and air. Islanded.
From the boat he'd
watched the ants run, time and time repeated,
to the edge, to the edge of their world,
as if looking for an exit from its ending,
as if in panic; when a leaf-
boat brushed, just once, against the dead-man-tree,
three ants jumped, at that instant, at it, two
fell and were swirled turning
down into the muddy eddies of the drowned things.
One
of the three ants made it to the leaf
and was last seen, rushing from one side

of its boat to the other, sailing
as if to discover   AntAmerica
already settled, a colony
to join onto? Ready to jump
if a moment of landing
presented itself.   Opportunist
as some humans
were not.

5

Ahead, what the ant came to –
was only a beat-up white weatherboard church
that the water sogged into, and ambled around,
inside and out, slowly, unmusically, apathetic
as an end-of-the-day stock horse.
If you can't
create an objective correlative, in music,
for your images …
if you haven't   enough
creative imagination   in you …
you'd better get out, give up
your scholarship.

(All his *études*
were eye-pictures
that his ears
got wrong.   His tonal compositions
were banal.)

The pantomorphic
nature of water.

You could count
the shapes it fell into,
never the substance.
Put water in glasses,
litres, tonnes:
you count the measures;
there is always water
water uncountable
inside them
outside them.

He
had made nothing
for water.
Even Pythagoras,
that ancient
picker and piler
of pebbles, that
ingenious mechanic,
discovered, with string
and mathematics,
something durable
for music:

The full string
sounds the tonic.
Clamped at 3/4, it sounds
a fourth higher.

This shortened string
is now clamped at
2/3 of its length, sounding
a fifth higher still.
The final length
is half the original
and sounds
an octave above it.

The out-of-tune piano'd
been moved, from the church, on the
back of someone's ute
on the last
Sunday before the
drowning. They'd not
played Debussy on it, found him
somehow wrong...as Gilbert and Sullivan...
were endlessly right,
for the church music society's
musical socials.

6

La cathédrale engloutie
he had found, had found him, last year
at the Conservatorium.
Once tears
have run, down a face,
they too

are uncountable.
The waterbirds had screams of murderers
and draggle-dipped their legs
as if to wash
a victim's blood off
as they flew. Uncle James
the local maniac had been discovered
screaming when he'd stepped, protected in the
cloak of his madness, into the iced white
winter river
to wash the sticky red off feet and axe. His banal – sane –
reaction
to his body's struggling in ice
had uncovered his madness. Victims were close.
Like a grotesque butcher-bird
he'd impaled their shortened forms
after death,
on stakes he'd sharpened
to receive them.

Was it an 'advantage'
to be related
to an axe murderer; if so
it was one he'd not looked
to uncover.

Uncle James
was a fact
he'd buried almost longer
than he could remember.

Age five, age six, age seven –
somewhere there.

There were no such
marks, going down, into the dammed valley,
to measure its depth.
A year ago when he'd jumped
out of the boat, to imagine better
the spires rising, the sounds
of the bells ringing, underwater, he'd had
to hang, clinging, to the boat's sides,
could not touch bottom.

7

Mist
passed overhead and rested
itself on the ground, wandering like a sick animal
getting up, lying down, all night.
Like a dog
he'd had that was hit by a car, that dropped
and struggled up, all through
the dark, as if it were afraid
if it stayed down
it would be dying.
On one side through the morning's clouds
there was a thin strip of gold light as if
the weather might be clearing. When he got
to the place far out

where the smoky cloud and the light rain
blurred the boundaries,
he was going to take
his transistor off, place it carefully
inside the holey doiley of his sweater
in the bottom of the boat, then
he was going to find the drowned cathedral.

~

When water fills your ears
and you hear nothing
you have a few moments
in which to try
to imagine

~

how to make
the unbearable
sound

Paisaje con un Pájaro **or Painting in a Wren?**

Green whiskers curl across
the world outside
as if they were a screen.

Happy as a person who has left
a dark & reeking saucepan
behind, in a burntbean-flavoured kitchen,
I have climbed here to the almost-top:
it is as dark as the water soaking
in a saucepan
in which green beans
boiled, burnt & started to stink.

The voice of a male blue wren
light as the rubbing together
of the legs of a stick insect
chirrs in the greenblack foliage
of this tree.

A webmaker has trussed up
curls, coils, canoes of bark,
in a microcosm
of mosquito netting. Ants
climb at this level, twenty metres up:
it is their highway, right to the top,
& the blue wren

hops along their path
flicking his tail as if
he were on a private
trail, through the brush.
                                        If you do not move
the ants will walk on you too
navigating agilely as if you were a part
of the ranges & valleys
of some mountain. They do not bite.
You are so still
blue wren takes you for tree
but sensing something awry
at the last
he gives his tail
a quick pleat
& scatters himself upward
into the blue air
that is too close
to be called stratosphere.
Parts of him are as blue as the butterflies
that drift down
through the tree's spaces, after him.
You were hoping
he would strut right up
& sidestep
flitting out on top of you.

Looking for Some Tracks (instead of making them)

The best poem you have ever written
hides like the Emmaville panther
dark/ myth/ uncomplicated by existence/
in a huge blackberry tangle
up the valley
beside the river.

You can hear it cough,
hear the dry snarl
as it moves its slight
animal's bulk, over sticks,
in the thicket's middle.

When your heart
stops pounding panic
& slows to an even
beat, you walk closer
& find the cat-tracks — entering or
                                        leaving? —
larger
        than any you have ever seen.

You cannot tell,   still,
with your nose stuck into spoor,
the tracks going into the thicket
from the tracks going out of it.
You've always been

a bad
reader of signs.
The surreal   has been padding
to & fro
tearing up
the ground all night.

Your poem, like the panther,
fails to emerge.

Giving up
on the idea of hunting
a poem as if it were
an animal,
going home
through the ordinary scrub,
towards Emmaville,
your head
lost in abstraction,
you meet an
unimaginative, non-drunk,
bush-walking,
disbeliever-in-panthers

who describes to you
in hair-crisp detail, perfect
down to dimensions of paw-print,
the objective correlative
to your unseen panther.
It is now

his panther   quietly padding off
to kill some sheep
over in Deepwater.

Perhaps once   a pair of panthers
did fall,   out of a travelling
circus truck (springing
out of their cage
that was smashed
by the accident)
& escape   into the real bush
round Deepwater or Emmaville?

You will be unable
to make your mind
move your feet
from the blackberry tangles
round the bad
simile of the panther
for at least
the next week.

Rear Vision

At Swansea under opaque sky
on oil-scented water of pearl-shell
a sextet of outsize people
are rod-fishing out of a boat.

Two of the fattest stand up and tip
like topheavy fruit in slow motion
out of the small boat-basket.
Which rocks. But remains upright.

Their muscled arms knifing through water
two fallen pear-bodies stroke for the shore
where grandmother waits toothless.
Her pale brown-blotched hands
flutter like bogong moths. She flaps
beside a rust-coloured ranch-wagon
which she has just moved
on to the bridge, to be closer
to the two in the dangerous water.

Looking forward in the rear vision mirror
you can see her behind you. You are helpless,
her mouth opening in a silent O.
Shark fins also
cut air, after prey, in these waters.

Though a mind's dread of shark
may fill a sea with blood,
the water stays pearl.
                    The next car
smashes her off the road.

An Impression of Minimalist Art in the Late Twentieth Century

A yellow
semi-deflated balloon
floats trapped
on a small
green circle
of water surrounded
by white
water lilies. Jagged
reeds fence the outer
water circle of it,
making palisade. Wind
would stretch
this balloon's rubber luck
thin as a condom
around nothing, pressing it up
against the submerged
pricks of the
flattened
fallen palm fronds.
It breaks with a soft
plosive,
sigh or an exhalation,
leaving no children.

The burst balloon's rubber
drifts slowly

down centuries of water
past the forms
of the swirling eels
and the sucking mouths
of their skinny offspring.
Going down without a self
through the centuries
it is seen as a yellow flower
or a floating petal
on a water lily garden
at Giverny. In the late
twentieth century,
it's ok, don't cry;
it is rubber!
Perfectly hygienic
to wear against the skin
to suck
or to throw away.
Ego leaves a mark on it
redundant as the whorls
of the first,
artist's finger prints.

Whistling the Fluff

When a dandelion's seed-head
is puffed off its stem,
by the shove
of a human's
blown breath
or a wind's
gusty exhalation,

the white fluff on
each seed

sails out
on top
as a wind-catcher;

the seed drops down
                                        beneath
like a nude brown person
    descending
        by
        P
        a
        r
        a
        c
        h
        u

t
e
the sky-well.

Naturally
when a seed
gets his/her feet wet
by landing in a
damp soak
or the black
ooze by a lakeshore,

the seed's feet
stick
and root
                rummaging round
in the lake
                    for sustenance.

The stuck
transmogrified seed
if not
taken out
by some
gutblocked Duck of Chance
becomes part
of a whole new
green generation
of wind-, earth-, and
water-pushed,

waving
wild

gold-flowered
weed dandelions.

The fluff,
that insignificant
insubstantial stuff

that powered the flight
by catching wind
when its passenger couldn't,

becomes that part
of the dandelion's history

that's destroyed by weather.

worn money

everything   is for burning
even & particularly
those things which most
                                        casually
you'd think to keep...

was the taker
nude when he
or she
numbfingeredly unhitched them
from the line
through the black
frost over Narrabundah?
did his or her
feet & hands
burn
with the cold?

David Brooks'
new jeans
fresh
from their first wash
drying out
on the iced
clothesline
in the black
frost over Narrabundah
travel out

on the hips of the unknown
swinging into morning:

fresh from the Mint
a fifty dollar note
passes out
into that great
mindless
adventure of
being: a stiff
crackling
thing of new currency

~

& who
will take them
from the taker?

~

jeans too
can pass
out of circulation
like worn money
slipping
into furnaces
on the
          withdrawing
hips of the dead

Slugs Could Ski

Excluded   by their otherness
from human
revulsion
compassion
or distress

if slugs could ski
they could do it

on the slime trails
from your
nostrils
to your lips.

This ground
is raw. It burns
where the
ski trails
cross it.

A handkerchief's
broad snow-plough
would drive
the agony in

sending in
an unfeeling

scraping Monster
like *NeverEnding Story's*
rough-edged Rock Eater

to clean up the trace
of a small
messy skier.

That the agony
going
down your face
is part of your cold's
(slow-beginner)
skiing away
is of no consolation.

One look
at the Am-o-lin's
gross cream worms
squeezed out lined up
set hard with winter

that have to be
rubbed in –
to heal –
's enough
to set you screaming

It takes Blue Jay
moving low

near the spindly end
of a saggy bough
                                        curling
his song out

round the pinkwhite
                                        dipping
tutuskirted blossoms

of the eucalyptus *leucoxylon rosea*
his territory – overhead –

to snatch your rage.

Unable to taste
the water from snow

or to sniff the crush
of a eucalypt leaf

mistrusting touch
rejecting hugs

reduced
to three senses –
seeing, hearing –
and pain

of course you blame
your mother.

Your mouth open
ready to roar

your lungs gripped
in a wheezy bellow

your cracked lips
surprise themselves

opening on a pure
red cave

of silence.

Blue Jay above –
You hiccup towards him.

now if you could...

when the poem is finished
it is set hard
like a hot pour
of errant
Wollongong Crude
that's been, inadvertently,
trapped, flowed, slowed, cooled –
& impossibly surprised –
by itself – at itself – at finding
a roughcast pig-iron self –
in a part-cracked
one-off mould.
it is **too** set.
now if you could
you would
ruffle its surface up
poke a gum twig
where three or four
hot disturbed black
biting ants're
angrily rushing about
– there – for it to chew on –
into its mouth –
& plant a wad of pliant
drawl-enriched
minty-green chewie
somewhere about

that an imaginary hand
has just
removed, from an
imaginary mouth.

Woman as Jug/ Blue Lady Poem

A real thrillin' game
of the old fuckin' bull
I handed in today lady – the speaker
swaying on his way to get some
lifesustaining plonk
to put   in the empty,
jug-like, blue
malleable container, it being
half after four – p.m. – he
having 'signed off'
from whatever it was
that he'd
                done – that he'd
dismissed – with such
mustard-mouthed self-derision.

Stout baby pigeons with stubs for tails
& shoulders built like sumo wrestlers
scatter, street-smart,
                                        from the weaving,
mocking course
            his squash-a-bird-or-kick-it feet
might take – with viciousness –
over the Neild Avenue pavement. He

is heading roughly for the Cross & it's
too near for him to be sober-

sour – when he gets there. It was he
bashed in a glass
& timber door – late one
moon-away, bleakish night back in winter –
his need   found a backstreet's junk – a
part white-ant-rotted spar of timber –
he used that – to spring his force through
into a renovated chicken shed where he
bashed you from your handbag, with its
food-money – thirty dollars.
(Another real unthrillin' game
of the old fuckin' bull,
that night, blue lady?)
Subliminal
glimpse, in a smash of glass,
he lives – like this? – & also
heaving bricks through car
back windows/ seizing/ by accident
of finder/ heroin stash in a worker's lunchbox/
cassettes – or better –
cash – to fill the thirsty mouth
of the mute & docile
greedy blue container.

All his seasons are in it:
whether it's empty or full,
Eyes say – he's not worth a song – ;
he makes his own: singing to no one
dancing to nothing.

When its mouth's full,
mouth to mouth, he & it
sway together, fucking deep,
having their own
bitter party...

He'd spit   in your sheep-stupid face
if you offered help – food, a bed – money –
            & bash
you blind when your back
was turned – to steal
                        some
of what you'd offered. There's too
much anger – & raging pride – for him to ever
get   what the blue jug wants
except by raiding for it/ smash & grab/
against the world/ or perhaps –
if he could find one to gull – by conning
a holy innocent.

One day he'll thunk a person dead:
unless   he does   extra well by it,
he'll not remember killing anyone.
Not a crease   on his paper face.
Not a scratch   on the blue lady.

All his reasons live in the jug.
Empty or full is the only weather.
If it's full, it loves him.

It is
his blue
lady of the air
& true
to him only.

Navigating Around Things

On the still
windless
Monday ground,
under the park gum,
clustered round its foot
& round the raised
roots of its toe-bones,

like a flock of creamy birds, crouched
heads down,
faking – eating grass seeds,

a motionless flock
of crunched cardboard cartons,
abandoned hollow
by the weekend's visiting humans. Galahs

navigate around this artefactual flock,
eyes only
on what is relevant to galahs. They

are stripping seeds, from the last
brown ears
of the summer's grasses.
                                        Nearby
horses canter fast & crisp, cutting

the humans' cricket pitch
with their shod hooves,

as if they were clipping scones
from the rolled green dough
of its cosseted grasses.

They are making frost breaths
in the ovens of their bodies.

Steam huffs out
in whitish wisps, ahead of them.
Pungent hot-baked horse dung
snorts out at the other end.

Chunks of turf
're flung sideways
when they gallop, sodding an innocent

downwardly mobile, young professional
on an 'indefinite
unpaid vacation' – from a job

with a broking office; not at all
suspicious he's been

'floated', on the air current,
outside a high-up window,
like a Kleenex with snot on it, he's

wistfully taking pictures
of any kind of action,

from the kneeling posture – worshipfully close
to the lovely risk of the hooves –

with a pre-crash bought-in-Bali camera.

Eels glide, down in the emerald murk,
sidling up to the light, swaying
like live, delicate arms
severed from dreams
of Balinese child dancers.
They suck, & wave – & terrify
the ducks. The only music
a soft 'fuck' as their mouths
take a bread morsel downward.

In the season of the small ducks,
when these day-old downy venturers
first stagger
                    onto the lilyleaf plates,
                    & wo
                            bb
                                le
                                  off
                                      raw
                                            live
into the astounding
                                truths of the water,

the large eels suck like centripetal force
that drags the water
out of the bathtub
                    & suddenly
in the dying dark
alone down an eel
goes a trustful fluffball.

Out on the lake, now – two
late-autumn duck parents,
calling mistrustfully.

                    Out
of a brood
of perhaps thirteen,
they've one
impulsive, casual,
jauntily-angstless survivor.

A small
sliver of moon
pale as a paperbark flower's
ghost spider
floats on the late-
blue, pre-dark sky – a moon
fraying at the edges
into wisps of white
like a child's worn-out
cotton undergarments
a moon

like a ghost child
of a grown moon
that is waiting
for its spirit's
next stage.
At the edge
of the moon, the sky
holds the
almost-rinsed-clear-of-colour
risk-dipped blue
tints of a bird's egg.

Incomplete Observation of Process

The brown rocking-chair
of the dove's tail
thrusts hard and regular
against the air
when dove
alights. (This rocking
is common to both sexes.)
As dove's feet grip
the steadying branch,
the rocking-chair loses momentum
becoming merely
a wedge of cinnamon feathers.
            There is something about
the way the chair rocks – at the beginning –
that reminds you
of mating. Thus when the chair slows –
and the rocking decreases –
it is like a sex drive
that runs out of 'puff' in mid
                                        act/ air/ art,
becoming oxygenless,
gasping,
running backwards from
completion.
              When
a male dove courts, he pursues –
cuckcuckcuckoo –

the female
to the edge
of the branch, shoving –
with menace of a
burly, disobeyed,
holstered traffic cop –
his portly body at her, till she
is pushed off
into space, takes flight,
retreats. A male
dove will pursue
the vanishing lady
with every line and centimetre of his body –
as a male painter might
the achieving of his masterwork:
my lady's *portrait*? – *cuckcuckcuckoo* –
she is his obsession.
Watching, you would think
female doves
shrinking, retreating, evading
had nothing
in the genetic heritage
of each one's life 'plan'
but a 'plot'
for individual
genetic annihilation: *they* pursue
the single life with as much
apparent
edgy fervour
as the male doves pursue *them.*

Turtle-doves *seem to mate*
when the male wears the female's
evasions into exhaustion, rather than
as a coming together
out of mutual lust. He tramps her hard.
She gives herself
a bemused shake as if to make sure
she's still alive and everything's working,
then heads
straight out into the blue
disappearing so fast
that the male dove, left behind on the branch,
had he a brain like a human's,
might've imagined he dreamt her.

How the nest-syndrome
fits in with all this
it is a little difficult
to determine.

                        A more
'open' vantage point
from which
                     to 'draw'
some further
'telling observation'
might perhaps
                        be that
of a sucking louse
on whichever

of the doves it is
does the nest construction:

… the sucking louse…
unbeknownst to itself…
always at risk…
when it's down
under the cover
of a feathery phrase
sucking lifeblood

a beaked head
reaches round
tweaks reprovingly
and squashes it.

They Do Well

Watching the pears'
soft life-bruised skins
vanish
inside red-whiskered bulbuls
you realise
what good bodies
the skins came from;
white sweet juice
is flung out
by the stabs
of each beak.
Great shuddery splashes of pear
darken the timber
deck beneath
as if
as they are eaten
the pearpeople are weeping
– spare my wife
  spare my child
  spare my husband
  spare me spare me –

Tears or blood.

Pearpeople's guts are gone
& the bulbuls show no mercy.

A 'mechanic'
at ripping out
the gut
of a bogong
moth
or a cicada
is a bulbul.
Bold. Restless. Quick.
They exist
outside the world of their Latin name
or the language's conceit.
Whether it is
a passive fruit
or a small
wind-shivered moth they take
& metamorphose
is a matter of indifference to them.
Pragmatic non-linguistic
survival mechanisms, they do well
in an urban wasteland
upon which sprout tufts
of hesitant trees.

Pycnonotus jocosus.
Introduced
resident of Sydney.
Black crested & scarlet bummed.
Acquisitive-eyed.
Beak like a pick.

At dusk
if you dim your ears
you will hear the dead moths turning
& the dead pears singing
as the bulbuls sing.

Chorus & Protagonists

Over
Centennial Park –
where Patrick White
used to walk – above
where he wanted
                his ashes blent –
in the middle distance, black birds
flap & wrap themselves, as if
round invisible lumps of air. They look like
bits of coal-sheeny washing:
wind-caught undergarments from Greek tragedy.
Cah, they cry, they are both
chorus & protagonists, as they swoop & flap
their underclothes of death
low over the
small birds darting into the tea-tree thickets.

At dusk a different
conspicuous villain
sits in the huge fig, he is black
with a white-tipped tail, gold
rings round his eyes like a gypsy.
Casually swinging from the tip of his beak
like a silverblue sardine
he has stabbed from the blue
tin of the air, he holds, before taking up

to dismember, on the upper branch,
before the student-audience, his three
gawky ignorant fledglings,
one perfect
Dusky Wood Swallow.
The class is Dismemberment 1 (Life-Drama)
for about-to-graduate Currawongs.

For All . . . (1987)

for all
the human animal
's ability
to web its world
with the structures
of its thinking

no human really
knows why it dies

any more
than a beetle does

half a world away
under the Europe-winded sky

picking insects
on the ground of Scotland

some grouse have already
taken in
their deaths and die

swallowing insects swallowing fallout
from Chernobyl

pecking they have caught
their part of the death of the earth

swallowing
are swallowed up in it

innocent as the children of Poland
eating food drinking water
from their deathrich Polish earth

as the children of Australia
eat fruit jams from Poland

as the peoples from Europe
eat foods from the lands of Europe

and drink   from the river supplies
Chernobyl fell into

as the produce of Europe
is loaded into scalebright schools
of container-fish ships

and insectwinged aeroplanes

to travel out   half a world

away   from the Europe-winded sky
to feed the peoples...

From HIV to Full-blown...

Moths blown away
from their deaths in the high country
die on the coast.

He will go, with his tears & his
typewriter, down below,
& type one more poem out
that he doesn't want to write.
His lover cannot hear it.
He is writing for those
of his friends still alive.

To them, he types, very slowly –
because his arms are shaking
& his skin
has the night-sweat fever:
All the faces you love
will become ash or dust
if only
you can wait long enough...

He has waited enough.

with the last of the light

twenty metres up
late-feeding white cockatoos
hang upside down
contorting themselves into banana shapes
to rip the orange palm-fruit
with their beaks

dog pee & duck piss
pull a dog's nose to the grass

the beak of a yellow-winged honeyeater
clicks sharply together as it
snaps again & again
on the trail of late insects

runners heave
asthmatically past
& toddlers' dreaming eyes beg ducks
to stay forever by blobs of bread
but the bread goes down too fast
it is all gone
& the ducks go with it

almost dark   a black swan claps
his wings' white undersides
on the water like thunder
the length of the lake

taking off   for the night's
black flying

with the last of the light
a professional sleeper-out beds down
claiming for the night
by being there
the metre-thick nest
that is softer than a swan's
under the pines
in the resinous den of needles

he has hessian bags
to cover his head & his face
he may fly
over any earth he chooses

hovering loud as helicopters
mosquitoes
looking for bare flesh
bald skull a bloodfuelled ear
or vein-blue wrist
round his warm
sleeping form
whine but cannot reach him

The National Glue – What Goes Down...Must Come Up?

If the nation's
glue
is too strong,
and you lick a lot, it will
make you sick. (Work
for Australia Post, you
will find this out.)

Or work, in your head, with your
imagination, working out
the how

of the rise of
German nationalism, concurrent
with the rise of
Adolf Hitler, and the Nazis: this too
induces nausea,
the manifestation of which
a doctor calls: vomit, a physical
law of the gut.

Or, have in your hands, the protest letters
of a class of primary school children,
which they want
lick-sealed
and sunk
in a letter-box...

~

Seven sheets of A4 paper
are strong enough
to break the leg of a pin.

~

In the context
of a contest between forces,

it is the strength of the paper
which snaps the pin;

the strength of the writing
on
the paper
                is irrelevant.

~

Though it varnishes your tongue
to perfection,
the glue on the new stamps
is too weak
to hold the perforated,
butterfly-wing thin, white
paper edges down.

~

Whether it is
two centuries'
accumulated guilt,
over a buried
theft,
of Australia, accompanied by
unacknowledged, unpunished murders,
or too much swallowed glue,
what goes down, must come up.
La Rochefoucauld's
law – of the vomiting psyche.

~

The 'artwork' on the stamps,
two,
crudely drawn,
blue and pink,
'thick' Australian children,
complacently turning
their fat faces
towards the 'celebration'
of Australia's 1988 'birthday',
embraces theft warmly,
by calling it something else.

The stamp design denies
white id its right to vomit,
black psyche its right to rage.

Or even to acknowledge, haul up, look at
what was done.

~

On the stamp, two
heavy, blond, Aryan-looking children
anticipate greedily munching
gross wedges of bicentennial cake

as many of the real,
pink, yellow, brown,
olive, white, dark-
skinned children from the many
cultures in this primary school,

do not...hot-faced with modern shame
at ancient bloody acts
(familiar to them
as instant coffee or
hot water out of a tap).
Their recurrent views...express simply...
if it'd been me, alive then,
I wouldn't have...
stolen their land...but (a consensus)
if a spear came at you,
you would have to send one back...

~

The stamps
on the children's protest letters

lift off
and curl up at the edges,
playing an active
game to subvert
gravity, all the way
to the large
red prick
that belongs to Australia Post,
where gravity
wins –
false children's faces on curled-up stamps,
and envelopes,
go sailing – briefly twinned and flat –
down to bed in the
all-people's, unhistoric,
childish, contemporary dark.

Selected Poems

1995

Brindabella
A Shot from the Seventies

                    :blue
jewel beetle
                  fallen
in the water   fallen out
of the split
gut of the trout

caught slit & gutted
like an unfilled
fish-pouch sandwich
                                    raw
with bloodied gill & flapping head

red
trout blood on the rocks   the flies
picnicking/ dipping their feet

on the other bank
                              a grey lizard
sprints a green clearing
to land
           in the chosen spot on greydeadgum as gum
to freeze   for a quarter-hour

nearby
a dead fox lolls

with the wet silver slipping out his nose
/ he was shot
on the track of the

wood duck in the dam/ half-
way/ across the paddock/ half-
way to the
wood duck's young
                                        as he moved   across the paddock
he was old –
his brush thin, not well –

he hangs now in the poplar
ropestrung by that brush

flies make their reproductions
where he swings red in the sun

red & green
king parrots gorging
on green apples

high   four thousand feet up

Part Seen & Fast Disappearing

like mice
in reverse

radiators;

their tails
disappear

down holes

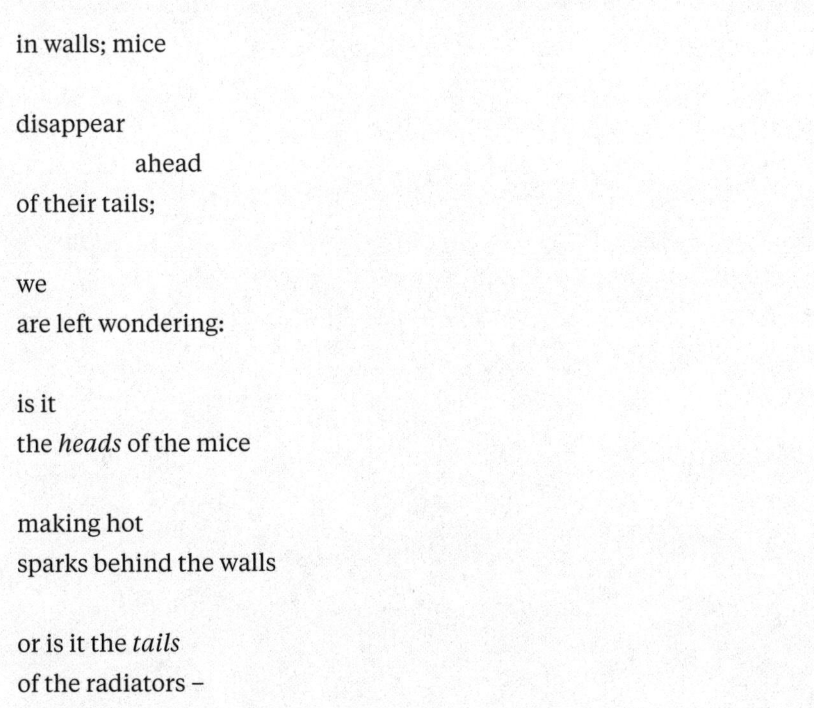

in walls; mice

disappear
            ahead
of their tails;

we
are left wondering:

is it
the *heads* of the mice

making hot
sparks behind the walls

or is it the *tails*
of the radiators –

plugged in
& the sockets faulty –

LOOK! COME QUICKLY!
THE ANSWER IS BURN1NG

heads or tails:
which *question* was it?

Mousepoem

Her lover departed
to the warm purry
bed of his wife,
with pale blue hands
in the cold dawnlight
she has written a poem so slight
she thinks if a mouse breathed on it,
it would collapse (the
poem, not
                        the mouse which is made
of tough, mouse material, whiskers, ears,
small, quick, risk-assessing eyes; the poem
is so light it seems to float, not stand;
the mouse…stands on firm mouse-muscles
& potato-crispy, cat-delighting
bones.) Who would ever   think of fucking
a mouse, but its lover? Who would ever
want to be fucked by a mouse but another?
Who would wish for blind, hairless
mouse-children, but a mousy mother?
Does a mouse wish
or are children merely what happens to it
wishless but wanting?
Time: is a moment
a mouse at rest? Pick it up? You cannot.
Relativity (by neither Newton's nor Einstein's
mechanics): when a human moves

a live mouse refuses arrest.
Even a blind mouse
will feel the great weight
of a malnutritioned
skinny human
& dart for the soot-stinky hole
behind a dead fire's
cold grate.

What has her slight poem
to do with a dead fire?
Ah...

Behind the Slice

The whine
of the butcher's saw
chewing its way
into the bones
5.30 a.m. Saturday.
Does sleep
have a body?
The butcher's dreams
of sleep 're transposed
onto the carcass of a sheep.
Half-asleep on his feet
he says he often dreams
he is the sheep – but alive –
and somebody else
is doing the cutting.

A Page for a Lorikeet

If
you are lucky enough
to have, as good friend,
a female   rainbow
lorikeet, she
will have two toes forward
& two toes backward
on each of her feet. i.e.
she will be of the older
form of bird, non-passerine.
Her toe-nails, minute, the
cloudy, tawny-brown
of combs sometimes made
from turtles hauled from the sea,
turn firmly, sharply in,
on whatever they grip.
Lorikeet toe-nails leave thin
scratchmarks   like delicate
birds' writing – nib
of a metal pen dipped in pink –
on the pale
skin of a human
leg, arm, hand, or wrist. Your
bark is skin;
they walk you as their tree...
it is here...i climb...it is here...
i cling

If she lands
on the front of your face,
she will have to sink
her beak & toes
into the flesh of your nose
& dig in, aiming for bone
to get a firmer grip.

If she climbs
the next
more dicey bit,
sometimes unnerved,
with one foot
resting lightly on
one of your awkward,
open, oddly-spongy eyes,
she'll stop –
unable to move
for panic.

You
at this distress
may choose

to offer her
an arm as a branch of escape

& she
may choose
to take it.

If she has made it
up the vertical   to the
tussocky, grippable hair
she too   is very pleased
& from her vantage point
tries to steer you eagerly
in the most suitable
north-south-east-or-west-erly
kitchen direction
which she will indicate
by rapid vehement nods.

You will be unable to see these
because of where she is.
Anyone else
will be able to read
& re-lay them too slowly for her.

Frustrated as a quick wit
trying to train a clot,
over & over, she will point you,
with her beak, to a
cupboard-caged,
crinkly, Savoy cabbage – for it –
instantly – to be lifted out; she wants
to play 'tough', quick! quick! jumping,
                    landing on top of it,
& ripping it up,

with her lorikeet beak
which is so good
at gouging
& at picking up
saucers, cups, dishes, flinging or pushing
them off shelves
for the floor to shatter,
at the sound of which she utters
gleeful, crowing screams.
                    These
will go on,
as shards bounce & scatter, becoming chortles,
if you're crawling innocently beneath her,
with your unsuspecting head down,
cleaning broken –
glassy mess – prime target –
with your
back *unguarded* –
to be landed on
for a rowdy play
or king-hit
by some prized missile
from her arsenal
of lids.

A rainbow lorikeet
that has grown up
around humans
will expect

that whatever she sees
you put in your mouth
will be good
for a rainbow lorikeet.
She will also expect
that you share it.

If you try to write when she
is out of her cage,
she will strut up to the pencil
& try to take it away from you.

If you put the pencil down
& play, she will not want
her game to include it
& will persistently entreat,
with inviting forward-nods
& intent, beseeching sideways-looks,
that *you*
should follow *her*
away from it.

Alternately,
if you have a sheet of paper out
when she arrives,
she will try – by lifting up a comer –
to get under it.

It is hard   to write
on a piece of paper
that has the energetic back
of a rainbow lorikeet   under it
pushing up at you.

The Sand

full of little holes
little tunnels

vacated by
little crickets

you hafta
go fast
to the head

of the tunnel

light years away
one will be there
somewhere burrowing

heading out

under the sand at the damp
bottom of the tunnel

there is this sound
like a note

along which
i am travelling
shaking

the sand off my legs
as i dig
tunnelling out

Public Private

2013

Drift

Her bottom –
like a Sherman tank?

What would *that* look like?

she's sitting
on a low stone wall

facing street.

It's a 1997
person, passing behind her,
who lobs the simile.

Those words,
directed towards
her flesh,
suggest a drift
backwards
into history Imaginations,
travelling out, dredge pictures
of Vehicles – Military. Mind as reader
runs through memory: *which*
famous Sherman
was the tank
named after?
How did it move?

Which model Sherman
was the passerby
thinking of?

However crude the simile
it's not a grenade, can't fall
back, upon the 1940s, (before
she was born) (where the tank's
action was)
real, with its pin out.

No simile
can smash one's bones
from its
machine-gun turret
or crush a human form
hers – or anyone's –
as the Sherman might have, once,
rolling casually on, leaving
behind
a death...

Wording
around anything
suggesting drift...thoughts
moving effortlessly forwards,
backwards,
sideways
into abstractions
quite bottomless.

Plop!

Kookaburras,
over a backyard pool,
carp   slowly vanishing.

Under round, flat green leaves,
gold-brown, murky,
blackish water.
are there
still carp?

Kookaburras. They are a family.
They wait for hours.
The youngest kookaburra
has not yet dived.
He cannot yet
make laughter.
He makes a sound.
Carp slowly vanishing.

Are carp infinite?

Are kookaburras?

What about humans?

Given dead humans
don't talk

given
the absence of a deity,

if humans
were not infinite,
how would the last one
prove, for certain,
she/he   was the last?

Finding a Destiny That Fits

Few
choose to suicide
by leaping into the pit
of the Manchurian tiger

as a young Chinese man
did
at Shanghai Zoo 4/ 1/ 85

Clasping
its jaws
over the young man's head
blocking
his view
of a banished world
the tiger
accepted
the offered life

Tiger, I will
be flesh of thy flesh

Afterwards
it was said
the young man
was of unsound mind

No one
doubted the sanity
of the tiger

Roost

the rain
making little
brown steps
on the roof
henlike
one
following
after
another

then the bees
arrived in the kitchen
clambering
round the weathered
edges of the crack

through the crack
behind each bee
as it climbed
you could see
a wide splinter
of the pearl-grey sky
some
early spring-

sun
behind it

you don't
need money
to imagine
the rain

making rooster-red steps
on the roof
over the kitchen

then
through the iron roof's
russet lace
                    on
                          to the floor below
              water
                   slowly dripping

The Earl of Rochester Rides Again or Open at Random

For five ninety-five, in the *Wormswork Classics*,
on the bargain table, at the Randwick Bookseller's,
nestling, between *Obsessive Compulsive Disorders*
and the shade cast by a hundred years
of the sales-power sun of Kipling,
you can wrest the Earl of Rochester
from his new nest,   half hiding (lurking?)
behind the skyscraper stack of Janet Frame.
                                        Open at random:
the Earl of R's protagonist Signior Dildo's chased
down the language's street – Pall Mall –
of London's seventeenth century

exhorted to 'escape!'
by the many…he has 'nurtured',

and pursued, perhaps to be kicked
into permanent sexual unemployment –

by a horde of pounding feet attached to pricks
of husbands he has cuckolded –
                                        who may
have it, in their swollen loins –
and ragefilled other parts –
to drag him
into some dark doorway
and stomp him out of existence.

You don't, in this
open-at-random, find
if the good Signior Dildo escapes.

(The Signior D.'s
a slim young swinger, fresh off a ship
from Italy, like that parcel
of foreign dildoes the English
customsmen seized, and burnt –
referred to in letter, to R, from Savile, penned
round sixteen seventy.)

You don't,
John Wilmot, Earl of R, implies,
need a carrot, a candle or thumb,
if you've good Signior Dildo in your bed.

Later, the Earl of Rochester's verses,
perhaps penned '*suivant la vie*'
in innuendo's deadly play
round the court of a decadent king,
roll from my lover's critical lips
as he reads aloud, between gusts
or snorts of laughter, and 'yes',
the Earl of Rochester rides well
in a late nineteen nineties bed.

Going back, with just enough
in the bald split purse
to get an extra, for a friend,

three days later, I find – in Randwick,
of the Earl of R – *Complete Works* –

there's not one copy left.

Over three hundred years
since John Wilmot
last laid down
his sword, his penis, and his pen.

Past Politics East Coast Crude

Say anything
to win, m'boy,
and afterwards we'll see
if we can come good
with a few
bacon rinds
for the 'ham'
of y' promises.

Whatever the size
of the next fella's ham
before the election
say what y'hafta
to make YOURS
look bigger heftier –
doesn't matter –
later
when y'r in
yer treasurer
'll strip
the wasteful
minorityinterestskin
and trim
the porky
party platform fat
off the 'beast' y've promised.

He'll pop it in his costing oven
and bring it out –
well-cooked –
cooled –
dried –
shrunk –
a twentieth of
promissory size –
no matter –
a sniff
is as good
as a feast
of smells
to the hungry, m'boy,
and sure

we'll all be that

after a bit
of time's
gone by – and things
've got worse
as we knew they would – course y'll hafta
throw us a few choice cuts
after y' get there –

with a lean beast
y' get less meat

whoever is
doing
the carving,

know this –

y' being
run
by the country.

Poem for a Person Who Says 'I hate poems that start with, use words from a language I don't speak.'

Le toit de l'aube
ou
sur un toit à l'aube du jour

After
a night of freeze
when walkers' breaths
huffed white
in the black
air
above the street,
bumping down
like a tiny aeroplane
that's spent
all night
out in the cold
wrapped round
its pilot, brain
still half-asleep,
stiffly
an early
Morning Pigeon
lands
& begins
to test

the icy tin –
    the Roof of the Dawn –
with just-awakening
                cold
pink feet.

A Sketch of Lovers

At the outdoor cafe's table
we sit, **you** draw, **I** write.
Wind wipes **our** finished coffees'
paper cups
off the table onto the ground.
I bend & litter-minded
pick them up. **You** are engrossed,
& sketch the lovers;   **your** felt-
tipped pen catches **her**
fullskirted
bottom
provocatively
on **his** lap. **He** may
have a hard-on. Abruptly
she springs up, gives **him**
a smoking kiss & this
your drawing does not catch – too many
moves to shape them all
on the creamy page
where the sketches mount. **He** stands.
She feels
the warm   round
his ribs as if
to reassure **herself**
that what **she**'s
hugged when bare 's   still there & **he** is
beaming &

together clutching loved bits
of one another
they move off.
Your hand
moves fast to catch the feel
of the look
she had alone on the seat when **we**
first sat
together there to draw & write
& **she**
was waiting
for **her him**
with all
of Saturday
stretched out.
You turn
& smile at **me** & ask
to see what's on **my** page & then
we rise   & the rest of the day
stretches forward

drawing **us** too   down a wanted path,
towards a bed, the feeling
flesh that lives
by touch, the wet in **me**,
the hard of **you**, some condoms,
an unclothed
ached-for night.

Her night thoughts

Last night
she wanted to bury her head in him
and stay that way forever.
Why she loves
sleeping with her forehead and nose
resting against the middle
of his back's a mystery to her.
Why she presses her nose
into the skin to the left of his spine.
Awake   her nose
is not a problem to her. Sits on her face
quite quietly, mostly. Like all attributes
'donated' by genetics, all physical 'givens',
Nose is not
a feature of herself
upon which
she reflects, (except perhaps as a sensate tool, what it
evokes and tells, as it breathes in the world).
Why, then in the dark, push it into his back?
Warmth? She does it on hot nights too
when there's not
much air. Close, like that, body heat
from his smooth
flesh rising. Not
for scent: his back's
Niagara-Fall-ed, by the shower;
he likes to stand there for hours, all

soap's fragrance expunged, by the H_2O
which simple Chemistry
holds clear as 'colourless
odourless liquid'.
Sometimes he
likes to 'lose'
his nose in her hair's
black depths,
and when he sometime says
he'd like to 'lose
himself'   in her, (he means, by this,
something other than what
is gained, or lost,
differently each time
by coming with / in
a lover's body –)
to lose himself in something that's
ultimately beyond
all definition, and
unknowable.

In a Dry, Dreaming

Wheat farmers
in their season,
lands sowed
                    waiting,

all their money
banked, if

o
n
l
y

they could draw it

d
o
w
n

net black, in the balanced
ledger :   no longer
                    in the red:

that thin
white line

still high in the sky,

cloud:

their future bread.

Return to Baghdad

After the Fall of Baghdad

1. School Goes Back

Iraq, 2003

Trying to find a quiet
safe route
to the Baghdad Library,
where he hopes to find out
if he can access the internet
without using Arabic
which he's unable to read,
pronounce or write,
Peter hears four Iraqi children,
running near him,
down a long strip of straight
tree-bare ground.
It's hard – like a Northern Territory dry-earth road
he'd followed once ,
travelling bruise-pawed on it for a week,
not knowing where he was –
but not as hard to hop on as igneous-granite outcrops,
riverbed rocks,
                              or what Max calls
rocket-propelled-grenade-smashed buildings
bulldozed into roads.

It runs,
              between what once
                                          were joined-together houses,

Peter guesses. Now,
unblocked by walls
the desert winds blow through

& for a moment,
                    before the standing houses start,
he can see no other Iraqis.
The children 're wearing the bright coloured sandals
he's seen strung on strings in the markets.
          He went to a market, crouching hungry & hot,
close to a stall where they dangled above him,
this morning with Max & Braid.
          Cool. Braid said. Plastic's useful.
She'd bought a pair – Iraqi green – & put them on –
          I'll wear them too, she said,
when it rains & the streets turn to mud.
Max, who'd been gazing at her sandaled
un-blistered bare heels
& small, smooth-skinned, pink toes, did
one of his camel snorts.
          He'd disagreed, Peter remembers.
Boots'd be better, Max advised. It won't be 'cool'.
It'll get cold when the streets start to flood.
You'll need boots then
for getting round here, &,

he'd gazed down at his own
rock-ripped,
near-worn-out leathers absently, even more
if you're still doing wetland

& marshes research – you'll need
to keep heading south. Travel's hard down there – dry or wet.
A lot of it'll be on foot.
Basra's ... worse now,
the Shias ... his voice trailed off ...
He'd looked more than a little worried then, Peter thought.

The children 've reached the streets with
some dwellings standing, others not,
& scattered off-white rubble mounds,
camel-hump shaped,
that Max said were made
from piling up pulverised houses. Peter'd heard him tell Braid:
Iraqis & their kids were crushed into the stones here
during the battle for Baghdad. Reporters
who came weeks later, when it was safer, said they could smell
the deaths in the rubble then. You can't smell death here now.
        Braid had shuddered.
Three of these children are boys, Peter sees, with black short hair
white-capped against the sun.
They are not very big,
with small slim feet. Laughing they kick
rubble-dust sideways at one another
as they run.

The littler girl takes smaller steps,
& lags behind. They are calling out in English,
which Peter suspects they are practising, since it is not
easy to understand, to tell their father:
BIG NEWS: All Saddam's faces

have gone from the classrooms, along with
the doors & the windows' glass, & many
of their school books   have photos & writings cut from them
which some children say
the teachers took   since they
have not been permitted
to cut anything out of the books.

There are not enough books   for all of them
& there are no pencils ...

Friends are missing.
Ali, Hassan,
Rajid, Ahmad & Hossein have disappeared.

It is September, two thousand & three.
Teachers say UNICEF
will be giving them new books – some
to write in –
& there'll be desks & chairs to sit on
later ...

When will that be? Peter thinks.
When is 'later'?

Without books, or pencils,
how do they now practise writing?
Do they draw
the thin fine lines
of the Arabic letters

his paws are too clumsy
to make
                        in the air
or in the dust?

He too
                        needs a notebook,
his own
is nearly full.
                        He is squatting in a doorway's shade
till they pass.
                        It's an indentation just deep enough
to hold a rabbit, set in the street façade of a,
perhaps-still-
human-habited,
joined-together,
two storey house, street level windows boarded up,
against (what Peter's read explained as) the widespread
malaise of looting by those out of work,
                                                in Max's most recent
                                                'In Iraq' column
                                                published by the SMH,
                                                several months back.

The upper windows,
                        to which, Peter imagines,
only a Huntsman like Clifta
                        could climb,
are blocked differently, by heavy, dark drapes
                                                that shut out the heat,

as well as the dust & the light.
There are no scents of cooking
or CD music noises coming out.

Looking down, he can see
there are no tired carrots,
desiccated beans or
yellowing celery stalks
that humans didn't want – & that he
might eat – put out
below.

All Peter can smell
is the grassless shrub-less ground,
the stone scent
of the leafless food-bare dust.
There are no vegetables greening anywhere at these houses' fr
no trees for fruits at their backs, not even
an unchewably hard-trunked lemon.
No gates or fences.
If a mother opened the door behind him to look for
a child back from school, in one step
she'd stand on the street.

Now it's car-less.

The children & their father, still loud in English,
pass by a motor repair shop. Its roof has gone.
They peer in. Black twisted cars,
shards & slivers of glass. Shrapnel. No one is there.

Marhaba, near-opposite, mid-street,
from a cart pulled by a one-eared donkey
a man selling kerosene calling out in Arabic.
The children's father answers *marhaba*
& then, in English hello my friend
He, too,
needs kerosene,
fuel for a lamp & stove
when the electricity cuts out,
but   cannot buy it now;
he is ... too far from home. No one there,
his wife... killed... two months back... in a bombing at a market.
He's taking the children... for safety...
to stay at his aunt's... till nightfall...
then going back to work – he's hired
for a few days clearing rubble. He'll collect them after dark.
Children, even of the jobless poor, have been kidnapped from
these streets – for ransom. It was safer under Saddam.
He harks back ...

Peter wonders if Saddam is dead   like the Iraqi
Hamid & Max left outside the morgue

& what it means   to be 'inside'   'being dead';
        what no body
designated 'outside'
        knows.
He remembers how fiercely he'd told the Flowerbed Rabbit
long ago,
Nobody knows what it's like inside it.

He could not ask the dead Iraqi.

Wittgenstein , in a philosophy note book,
once wrote, when he was a private in the Austro-Hungarian Army,
& before he was imprisoned in Italy,
Death is not an event in life ... Peter's ears stiffen
as he remembers Wittgenstein saying (over thirty years later)
(for a man) 'at death
the world does not alter
but comes to an end.'

Peter's small body tenses with concentration.
He reasons.
The dead do not have a world...
A human's world is language: 'logic' & 'words', Peter thinks.

The dead Iraqi could not speak.
Those around are live, hence cannot know.

He can hear more car engines now,
& peering out, round the stone of the doorway, sees

more people using the street. He does not feel like venturing
towards the Library amongst them. He has not yet
discovered exactly where it is
nor – crouching lower,
ears flattened apprehensively – if he will have to cross
a circling motorway... cars speeding, to reach it or bolt, in dayligl
over a crowded Tigris bridge.
He decides to retreat

to Josh's house ... & perhaps work on
Anaximander, an early (a pre-Socratic)
philosopher, (who belonged,
Peter's read, 'to the Milesian school')

instead of the Islamic – & later – Baghdadi,
Ya'qub ibn Ishaq al-Kindi, who is the one,
on the Library's internet,
he wanted most
to research.

Pricking his ears & sitting up again
to look around,
                                        he sees the children
& their father turning left,
disappearing,
down a narrow smoke-filled alley.
Where they are heading
he cannot see & does not know that ground. Above him,
high over the city, changing direction,

bronze pigeons curve in a turning circle,
their wings becoming iridescent as they wheel,
between him & the sun.

2. Returning to Josh's

After a second unsuccessful search for the Baghdad library
(which he does not know was burnt down
one week after the fall of Baghdad),
returning to Joshua Smith's,
Peter remembers Clifta ordered him
to search for another picture of,
& some 'facts' about, Bahram – all

without using the World Wide Web,

which she's convinced 's a bid for global power
by the St. Andrew's Cross spiders,

'species Argiope aetherea family Argiopidae',
a Christian set or sect

who're trying to extend their already huge,
white X-ed webs

far beyond Sydney –

a belief to which he gives no credence,
but from which – so far – he's failed to dissuade her.

Perhaps he can get onto one of the Iranian
web sites in English, using Max's old computer,
to find out about Persepolis – & the Takht-e Jamshid,

but it will need to be a time when
the Baghdad electricity's,
at least for a short while, working.

Persepolis may be where Clifta needs to go, by bus or plane,

to look for 'facts' about her... perhaps-ancestor... Bahram.

He remembers Clifta telling the story of
her mother's reading, to her & to the tiny siblings, Arachnid
        Fitzgerald's translation
of the poem in which the two names Jamshyd & Bahram were linked.
                He's begun to suspect,
through three nights' laborious torch-lit study of Braid's newest fat
        book, his paws
awkwardly turning the pages, the torch set in the 'on' position on
        the floor,
                that 'courts'
                have thrones in them, & that
                Takht-e Jamshid...
                may be 'Throne of Jamshid'
                in Persian. But, perhaps, as the spelling's different
                ('i' not 'y') the latter may be a different
personage – or person. Many humans, it seems, over time, have had the
        name 'Jamshyd'
            dropped upon them, or the version
                that crossed over into Persian.

He manages to move quietly through the cave-like front
of Josh's, skirting round the stairs to Mio Palazzo

without meeting its perhaps-still-grieving cat,
& cross the kitchen without Clifta noticing,
to reach the part
where Max & Braid have got themselves set up.

Braid's on the phone to Weasel Smith
telling him she's not coming back.
She doesn't love him. She's now 'with Max'.
Peter's ears twitch.
He can feel Weasel's Sydney anger coming through the Baghdad ph
Shout of: 'Shit you slut. I had a prostitute last night who had more c
    than you.'
Squatting quite close to Braid,
he hears the crack of something smashing & starts to move away...
Weasel says he's breaking
anything of Braid's that's in his Bondi flat.

'You'll never see the bound copy
of your environmental thesis again:
I'm going to throw it off The Gap.
Along with your new computer,
your secret stash of leaked documents –
about the Murray-Darling Floodplains dry-out,
& that fat... seven hundred & sixty page... research book
on-loan-from-Fisher you haven't... bothered...
or were... too fucking sloppy... to take back.
They're all going over The Gap.'

'You'll never work again as a journalist – without me.
I'm burning all your left behind clothes.'

Stringers need to travel light. Goodbye Weasel, she says quietly.
Cutting him off. She's temporarily without Max, in Josh's
(post-looting) bedroll, backpack, & cardboard-box furnished,
missile-damaged house.
Peter, who'd crept through an arch to the room next door,
to look in the chiller's vegetable box, while Weasel was still
in full roar, returns. He's been unable to open the kerosene fridge.

He remembers Max's gone to the airport, from there
to the press briefing session
to re-connect with some journalist friends
who are looking for news in the 'Hunt for Saddam'.

Most, he'd heard Max say, want stories of sightings –
even a passable look-alike –

some   want the capture
above a by-line
instant front page.
                        Max doesn't
...anymore...
(he said), but...
he'd   like   to see Saddam caught...

The Yanks, the Brits & the Iraqis
for not always congruent reasons
want his presence in their present.

They want him found.
They want him fast.

They are looking for him everywhere.

Reports coming in, hour by hour,
they follow up
any lead they've got.

Braid's fingers start to move again
on Max's older, backup laptop.
Peter hears the click of the keys & hops closer.
She's making notes – about the Tigris-Euphrates Delta Wetlands.
On stapled-together sheets of A4 paper by her side
he reads: United Nations Environment Project,
March, two thousand & three.
The day date's blurred by a splat of coffee.
She notes there's been   gradual   shrinkage   of the water,
since the war between Iraq & Iran that the report calls The Gulf War
& there are maps that show it.
It seems the Tigris & Euphrates – when they flood –
have been stopped from overflowing into the Wetlands, & the tides
have been blocked from overflowing into the marshes where the
  Ma'dan lived –
& the fish & the ibis –
& birds on their travels broke their flights to rest & eat.
He remembers, then, being poled past the woven reed nest of a
  Basra warbler
over murky waterways that smelled like wet-feathered ibis
& the warm dry scent of the gold reed basket in which he had crou
  to hide.

But Braid is writing about fish, he glimpses a French word on her
lecture pad
...*les disparus*... & looking away from the handwritten notes,
watching Braid's long slim fingers constantly landing & taking off
from the silver-grey keys of the laptop –
she is sitting cross-legged on the floor with it –
he edges forward, reads, HABITAT DESTRUCTION
then, not one but all   of fifty-two species of native fish
that lived in the Iraq Delta Wetlands   now   have disappeared.

It seems... that they are dead.

Braid is weeping softly

Peter wonders why

R.PHL

Hard as a Sun-dried Carrot ...

A group of Cambridge's scholarly professors
wants Peter Henry
to conduct a survey
of the 'reading & writing habits'
of 'The Australian Rabbit';
that this
is a collective term, which has been intended by them
to include at least three –
who're
'moderately literate' –

has been explained to him in their letter;

skimming their page which is
l
o
n
g
he notices they have underlined
CONDITIONS for his survey: some
of the 'rabbits'
need

to be poets, &,
amongst those

who are
    'moderately literate',
which of them
would be likely
to read
a History
of Philosophers?

Amongst the
Research 'Tools'
(which are different from those
on the Tool bar
of Max's computer here in Baghdad)
Peter sees they've listed – under 'useful' –
a book
by the critic, Queenie Dorothy Leavis,
first published in nineteen thirty-two,
that was written as something called a 'thesis';
Peter, who's been practising the one sign
he's learnt to make in Arabic, decides,
  from the Cambridge scholars' precis
  of this work,
he is probably not
that particular critical study's 'ideal reader'.

However, there are some factual parts of it –
hard as a sun-dried carrot –
concerning 'markets'
from which he feels
he might perhaps

learn what to do. She did, it seems, consult
the Encyclopaedia Britannica, & though
that work
has the reputation
for factual veracity,
he does not think
he would find even one
of its heavy tomes in the Baghdad Library,
since the Encyclopaedia Britannica has not, as far as he knows,
been translated into Arabic, nor,
if his relation Picasso Rabbit went to London
to look for the E.B. in a library,
its knowledge would tell him
how to do the research in Australia
& send out questionnaire-letters
to gain   replies
from readers there. Many writers
Queenie Dorothy Leavis wrote to
simply did not bother
        to answer
        her questions.

He thinks it might be hard
to locate, & coax up,
from its nose in a book in its burrow,
a 'moderately literate'
Australian rabbit
who's also a poet.

How, & where

is he to find
the readers & writers
for his survey?

Scratching one ear reflectively
he asks himself:
would
the Flowerbed Rabbit
know?
She's done some
research for him in Australia;
since learning to read & write, she's found out how to access
information on the internet,
though
        (Peter considers) she sometimes
        misunderstands
the questions which he wants her to tap in
        or else   the internet does;
most of the 'answers' she gets
seem to involve

locations & amounts
of recent precipitation (New South Wales only)
        hence likely locales
(there) for locating
the best, juiciest – only two or three day old –
new grasses.
        She seems to have stopped
getting answers
for his questions about philosophers.

She's also learnt
a way in, after dark
to use
some
of the books in a Wollongong academic's
personal library.
She got a lift there by accidentally falling asleep
amid a load of vegetables
on the back of an elderly truck
belonging   to a white-headed south coast vegetable farmer.
called Moon Tree
whom she later found out
was visiting a poetry-writing son
doing English – Honours – at Wollongong Uni.

This means nothing to Peter, since she has not told him
in her latest batch of letters,

forwarded to him c/– a pipe shop
close by a market where Max & Braid shop,
what she is reading, nor even
which of the vegetables she ate.
He hopes they were juicy –
not like this Iraqi carrot which has travelled a long way
by truck, to end like a red rock in the sun.
Perhaps it came from the Kurdish region.

He finds his right paw has drawn a firm capital N
followed by a smaller o, on the ground in front of him.

Some things are unknowable.

He cannot find out
what the Cambridge scholars want him to.
He does not think that the Flowerbed Rabbit
would want to try, nor that anyone
        could
find
        the answers.

He determines
        to affirm
        his willingness

to pursue his work on the History of Philosophers
        &,
very firmly,
                to decline to do the survey.

Another 'Smith' Story?

They are wearing metal
basins on their heads

that Max calls 'helmets'.
Peter is thinking

of a photo he has seen
on the ripped-off

front cover
of an Australian magazine

that Max
brought back

from the brief
research he did

last week
in Sydney.

This photo
is sitting

on one of Mormon Josh's
dates-for-export crates

in Josh's thirteenth wife's bedroom
back of the Baghdad kitchen

where Max & Braid have stored some stuff,
Josh, not minding, & anyway, being absent.

Why didn't you use the internet? Braid
wants to know. Max is sheepish.
He needed to sniff around...find out
if he could drum up any interest, Armistice Day coming up,
in an oddball piece he's thinking of doing –
& No, in answer to the unasked
question, & her anxious face, I managed to avoid
seeing Weasel Smith. I heard he's taking boxing lessons.
He says he wants to kill me.

Peter thinks Sydney is a long way from Baghdad.
He hops close, to re-examine the photo.

There are a lot of men
that Max has said are : 'Diggers'. What
have they been digging?

There is a kind of sepia trench
in which they sit,
play cards or smoke.

It is deeper
than the one Peter & the Flowerbed Rabbit found –

just before the Iraq War – that trench
chopped into red dirt
by a machine with a cutting edge so sharp
they didn't like the look of it. They heard it was
'excavation' – so that men could sink round pipes
to carry water
down a long straight road
to a town so far away they couldn't see it
somewhere near the centre of Australia.

A few of the men in the sepia trench photo
are lying very still.
Suspicious Braid leans forward
pointing with her finger: Are those two dead?
It's likely exhaustion, Max says, looking up from his notes, but no
at the ones she's pointing at.
Some may be shell-shocked, wounded or unconscious.
This was taken near Hill Sixty at the Third Battle of Ypres.
It was pretty bloody.

Seems they've been photographed by an Australian
called Sir Hubert Wilkins MC (& Bar),
who took the submarine Nautilus
close to the North Pole –. first anyone except perhaps the seals,
had gone under the polar ice cap to explore there,

& who, Max says, was famous also
(as was another man called Hurley)

for taking photographs of these Diggers

some of whom, including engineers
tunnelled underground
beneath the front line
that separated the two armies,
so they could set one massive mine,
& a number of averaged-size ones, way down
under the Germans' gun positions,
& detonate them all together

eighty-six years ago
near Ypres & a village called Passchendaele
In The First World War,
in nineteen seventeen,
in Flanders.

Wilkins & Hurley were there when this happened, Max asserts firmly.
The Allies, who'd been failing to win so far i.e.
to over run the Germans' gun positions
by killing enough of them to force a retreat
didn't exactly win that one either
though the explosion was loud enough
to be heard by the (then) British P.M., Lloyd George, in London.
The order was to Advance but they didn't have
dry sand for the tanks. There'd been
heavy rain. The ground was a quagmire.

Gazing down, skim-reading his hand written notes,
Max adds thoughtfully: Wilkins was also known (though not
well known) for
going into battles armed only with his camera

with (perhaps once ahead of) the first assault troops,
& for being
        many times wounded.

What's 'oddball' about that?
Braid wants to know. Journalists & photographers
have been killed during combat, in this war,
as well as wounded
        Where's your angle?

Max looks a bit disconcerted.
He was one of two
official Australian War Photographers
with Frank Hurley.
He was wounded nine times,
kept going back, to take
& develop
front line photos, even
after he'd been declared 'medically unfit' –
he'd been gassed, blown out of the sky
as well as had bones broken ,
many times over;

He got the Military Cross twice. They don't hand them out lightly.

I thought I'd get permission to republish
some of C J Dennis's old verses, printed
in nineteen eighteen, & brought out twice
by Angus & Robertson, Sydney, in that last

year of the war, the second time in handy
POCKET EDITIONS FOR THE TRENCHES

I guess the market died on them;
they couldn't know how soon the war would end
for Australian soldiers on the Western Front with
presumed trench reading-habits
nor when the remnants of the A.I.F. 'd return.

Peter who is squatting in a corner
inspecting some of the photos
watches Braid who seems to be waiting
perhaps for Max to explain further... He thinks
she looks a bit puzzled.

In one of the men-relaxing- in- trenches photos by Hubert Wilkins
        Peter sees
one soldier is looking at a page from a magazine
that has pictures of women with not many clothes on. Another man
is sitting staring at two unfolded pages
of a small newspaper.
(It looks smaller, Peter decides, than Max's
two thousand & three
New York Times or The Guardian Weekly).
No one had a book. No one else is reading.

Shuffling the other photographs clumsily with one paw,
tipping each one onto the floor, after he's finished looking at it,
Peter can find no signs of pocket-sized books in use.

When Max begins to speak again, his voice sounds dry, less intere
It's pretty obvious. The phrase
'handy pocket edition', suggests, I guess, motivation:
mums, girlfriends were to be inspired to buy the littler size
to send to sons, lovers, et cetera thereby enabling their loved ones
to carry something evocative
with them in their pockets, to read in the trenches.
& laugh or sometimes chuckle at the illustrations by Hal Gye.
There's a linked episodic narrative told though different blokes'
        viewpoints –
you'd need a glossary now to explain the slang – about 'life back ho
as epitomised 'round a struggling rural pair,
'Mar Flood' & her old man,
whose sons
        went missing
Some of it's moving, even ... quite poignant
At times bits are sentimental & bathetic. There's a mysterious laco
        returned soldier
with a missing part, a leg I think, left in France, who's suspected
            of working
some kind of con on the elderly Floods whom he ... pretends to kno

the younger son 'Mar' grieved over the most, it's hinted
was a tearaway, who

may have done a bunk from home to dodge
felt pressure to enlist,

to 'Mar,' embarrassingly
presumed
        'reluctant'
                to go to war,
some shame, the story's teller hints,
there was for her, in that,

the other referred to tearfully as
'Our Syd' was 'killed at Suvla Bay'

Looking back, it's sentimental stuff
for the ageing Australian still-newspaper-reading
population – or 'quaint' for the young
a window on a 'vanished or bygone Australia'.
Some literary editors still use that sort of stuff.
I don't need Weasel Smith to sell it for me.

It's called Digger Smith & dedicated to the A.I.F.

I thought I'd offset the Digger Smith poems, quoting some
of its jokier lines, as well as the grieving ones,
with Wilkins' nineteen seventeen trench-warfare photos
of a different kind of 'life' –
'when a million men faced one another & half a million died'.

I think I can connect them, & write 'a nostalgic feature'
to tie in well
with the two thousand & three,

eleventh day of the eleventh month
at the eleventh hour,
re-celebration
of Armistice.

Howard & the RSL will love it.

Have you got the book? Braid asks him doubtfully
Max grins triumphantly, pulling a small, green
clothbound object out of a small brown paper bag.
Peter, moving closer sees
there's nothing else inside the bag,
but a drawing of a large fork
standing by itself in the smooth earth, as if waiting for a human di
to plant the waiting potatoes, also depicted on the eighty-five-year
book's front cover.
Last trip back!
I fluked a second-hand copy
from a shop in Oxford Street,
near the Verona picture theatre. Weasel never goes there. He's
too mean to buy a book, for which I'm glad –
I didn't want to have to punch him in the guts & knock him flat.
He's older than I am – & none too fit.
Braid winces.

Journeys Digital – & 'Other' Worlds

A voice-over tells that since nineteen seventy-nine,
when the Russians invaded Afghanistan,
fifty-three thousand Afghan refugees
have come to live – where the film begins –
in Shamshatoo refugee camp in Peshawar,
close to the Afghan border, in northwest Pakistan.

Peter Henry Lepus hasn't been to Afghanistan, or
to Pakistan.
Scratching one ear reflectively,
he considers. The movie shows a lot of those countries'
brown deserts,
as well as some of the roads in Iran,
which Clifta may want to use her many eyes on –
if she is to look ... for the ground ... of Omar Khayyam,

whose Khayyam name, his father's, seems to mean
he came from a family of tent-makers.

A friend from those pre-Gutenberg times,
Nizam al Mulk, Omar's co-student,
wrote a 'memoire' of Omar
that Peter has read about
(the friends were sent to a Muslim scholar, an Imam,
to study the Koran).

Peter has also read that the Persian calendar
was re-designed by Omar,

who was ‘learned in science, as well as astronomy’,
wrote a ‘table’ of the stars, & an algebra book
that travelled to Europe.

The other of Khayyam’s two school friends, Peter’s found out,
later became
the ‘notorious’,
austere & frightening
‘Old Man of the Mountain’,
who, from a castle south of the Caspian,
developed the ‘Cult of the Assassin’,

about whom, & about which,
rumours abound,
        partly due
to the tales told
to an early travel-writer,
who visited the terrain,
about one hundred & fifty years later, recording what he heard
with pen & ink
as he did not have a camcorder, within a volume
titled: The Travels of Marco Polo.

Peter, who’s been searching more recent books
on behalf of Clifta, finds that Khayyam’s bones
are said to lie in something called a ‘Tomb’

        & that he died
in the first quarter   of the twelfth century

in an ancient Iranian city with at least
three spellings, the most recent of which

Peter's found, after many fumblings through old books,
seems to be Neishabur.

He has not found Neishabur yet,
on this movie's maps
which flash by fast
showing its journey's routes in red.

He remembers the little spider's telling him
of her mother, reading, in a Sydney park, aloud
to her & all the little siblings, 'Arachnid Fitzgerald's translations
from the Persian' – a poem which was recited to him
solemnly in the Iraqi desert many, many times;
the poem ran:
They say the Lion and the Lizard keep
the Courts where Jamshyd gloried and drank deep
And Bahram, that great Huntsman, the Wild Ass
Stamps o'er his Head, and he lies fast asleep.

Peter has not found out
what a court is, hence
what it looks like

There may be places in this movie that Clifta may feel

she needs to go ... if she's to 'find'
        Bahram, the great

Huntsman of the Rubaiyat,
whom she believes ... may be her ancestor ...
even, he thinks despairingly, inside her imagination ...
There may be digital videoed roads she wants to travel
in her search; he's seen an Iranian bus's red
Sydney-Huntsman-Spider-concealing curtains
that Clifta may want to travel on. There are cities, too.
Esfahan & Qom he has found, on his own
map of Iran, & they are 'represented' here on this movie's map
on a route to Tehran.
His long dark rabbit eyes
focus on Max's screen,
where play
of the DVD
that's been fast-forwarded,
has stuck. (Or is it merely stopped?) Braid says there are some scra
        on it.
They've watched the same scene several times, & jumped,
to Peter's surprise that a movie has them,
into CHAPTERS, (sequenced forward)
with long stretches of the movie's story
left behind.

The name   T E H R A N–
printed in large scarlet capital letters across the screen

points him to an idea. Planes fly to Tehran. If Clifta can get to
        Baghdad Airport, she
could perhaps stow away under a round white cap like the one
that Jamal wears, when he leaves Peshawar from the refugee camp

in northwest Pakistan, where the movie's journey starts.
She will probably need to fly to Tehran, to begin her search,
Peter thinks,
turning round to see if she is watching
any
of the movie's many roads or its fewer maps. He thinks she should be.
She is the one who said, I want to go to Persia, NOW.
And perhaps there may be people at the University there, who can
help her.
Peering under the table he sees she has crawled into a large crack.
There seem to be two of her. Then, he realises. One 'Clifta' is the
old skin,
thin, papery, that Clifta's left behind..
The new Clifta crouches wet & strange (estranged from herself?) inside
a larger skin
that Huntsman Spiders have to make, to grow. Her old skin was not
big enough
to hold her.

Humans, as well as rabbits, Peter's learnt,
live & die as one; they do not need
to change their skins, to grow up,
though all need food, 'safe' air to breathe,
& water…

The two young Afghanis on the screen have to change
their clothes – 'to look Irani' –
the caps they wore from Pakistan   must also disappear.

They try to learn to make new sounds, speak Farsi, not Pashtu.
Enayat learns the word 'snow' in English.

Is it cinema verite? Braid asks. What is that? Peter wonders.
He has seen the word 'cinema' written in gold,
high up in some cities , above crowded streets, on buildings
he has not been inside. He does not know what cinema is,
nor that *verite* means 'truth' in French.
He has not seen it written
on any buildings, whole
or hollowed out by what Max called 'Tomahawk cruise missiles',
in Baghdad, where he is now, nor has the word verite appeared.
It is over five months since Saddam's huge statue
was pulled down – & that act – & scene
turned into photographs,
& recycled, for money,
sometimes with enigmatic U.S. soldiers' faces
& a few close-ups of excited teenage Iraqi boys, & men,
with stories about the 'fall' of Saddam's regime
on newspaper front pages round the world.

In a hotel outside the Green Zone,
with a basement power supply
that Max has paid to use, Peter Henry Lepus,
Max, Braid, & occasionally Clifta
are trying to watch a DVD
which a journo friend of Max's brought in from London
that recently won the Golden Bear Award in Berlin.
Isn't it rather soon for it to be released as a DVD? Braid asks.

Max,
for once, is not listening to her. One arm
round her shoulder he says,

They used two Sony digital cameras, one left on all the time,
    & a camcorder.
It has the feel of a doco but it's facto-ficto. The route was travelled first
    by the writer & director who followed people smugglers routes,
    collected stories, & came back later
to shoot, sometimes using guerrilla doco tactics, to catch transactions
    in backrooms
between people who didn't know they were being filmed.
No script. Few pros, mostly those in it
played the story'd versions of themselves.
It's a distillation. People-smuggler experience
isn't pleasant.

The last scene is shot in a mosque,
which Max says was filmed in London.
The younger one, Jamal, is grieving at last for his friend,
his cousin Enayatullah
who got sick in a black space inside a box, where
Max says the oxygen ran out;
there was not enough 'good air' to last forty hours for the ship's journey,
which is marked, on the film, by a red line across blue, to Trieste,
from Turkey. The box is called a 'container'.
The blue, Peter's learnt, is what map-makers use
as a sign of sea or ocean:
if you know what it means, you do not need
to be able to read words; though, he has also found,
map-makers like to write words
    across map's blue,
    that tell   which ocean or sea   is pointed to.

Other people were travelling in that boat's black space ...
Afghanis, from the northwest ...
Max says they'd be defined as 'Economic refugees',
in politician or migration official English,
an old man with a beard, a woman & her husband with their baby..
They got sick like Jamal's friend
who was his cousin & arrived dead except Jamal & the baby Mehti,
who is shown, when the container's at last opened,
trying to put his mouth to his lifeless young mother's breasts.
Braid is weeping quietly by the ending.
Peter, Max, & Clifta who's crawling,
still damp in her new skin,
under a bench by the old iMac's table,
do not speak.

Max was in Doha recently
to watch some Al-Jazeera footage
of the Assault on Baghdad,
spent days, perched on a desk
watching interviews with grieving people
who'd lost mothers, husbands, daughters, wives,
sometimes all
of their families. After that, he watched
the later news stories
of the carnage that followed the
suicide bombers. An Iraqi driver he'd talked with
on his way back from Doha
'd been blown up,
just after he & Max had parted.

It’s time-out for me from watching replays of the real war, he says,
leaning back on the green plastic chair
to re-watch a movie that’s not showing either missiles,
a city sky line with buildings burning
or debris blown upward
by landed bombs. You’re hard, Braid accuses him quietly,
removing his arm, getting up, with the free encyclopaedic extract
from Wikipedia in one hand. She’s headed for the bedroom, to
        read about
the facts behind the movie’s making on her own.
Peter does not relax from his stiff squat.
Both ears erect as he watches what is re-screened,
he is thinking back to past images.
The film does not show him any libraries
that he might send Clifta to,
to begin to search for records by & for herself.
He is beginning to suspect
that ‘Bahram’,
Clifta’s ‘great Huntsman’, from the poem
‘Arachnid Fitzgerald translated’,
        perhaps from Edward
        FitzGerald’s very free, renderings
of the Persian of Omar Khayyam,
may not have been a Sydney Huntsman Spider
or even one from Australia,
&, in fact, may never have lived, hunted,
or gone to sleep,
anywhere within this world.

Braid on Braid

Braid decides,
she writes
on thin airmail paper,
she doesn't want
a child yet
with Max – he's too independent
& un-
'family focused'. She doesn't think
he'd make a good father yet,
not
the way he is now:
too much the
unencumbered
        single reporter,
disappearing
by air to Riyadh (Back in two days
followed by flight details)
without telling her
why he's going,
        (the absence   of his air travel bag,
cryptic as a note with read me on it
followed by invisible writing);

then, just talking of taking a trip
to northern Iran –
where the hot springs – & less active volcanic areas are –

round the east & west ends of the Caspian – which
she wants to write about   & has   talked with him
recently   about wanting to visit
to see how eco-development & tourism
are impacting on the wildlife, & if,
since two thousand,
there's been an increase
in sewerage pollution, in the Caspian,
if measures
are being taken to combat it.
If so, what?
but he hasn't   even asked her
if she wants to come with him.

Perhaps, she, too, needs to grow up
she confides, ending a
letter to
her widowed grandmother out from Mudgee.

Then, taking stock,
seemingly alone in the
semi-ruined house,
feeling slightly sick
& suspecting pre-menstrual tension,
Braid wonders what her chances are
of passing a recruitment office for new, post-Saddam-&-Ba'ath-
Party-appointed, police, on her way
to arrange the letter's posting

to her granny, of ending up:
        namelessly melded
with an unknown bomber & some equally-unknown-to-her:
randomly passing
husbands, fathers, children   & mothers

as depersonalised de-humanised   flecks of bone, blood & flesh
(not like the skinny sheep
her granny routinely drives in the back of a ute
to be illegally slaughtered
& sold in a rural home-made-pie shop in Australia)

but right here   on a Baghdad street.

Index of Titles

Acknowledgements

The poems in this selection have been drawn from the following original collections by J.S. Harry, whose publishers we acknowledge: *The Deer Under the Skin*, University of Queensland Press, 1971; *Hold, For a Little While, and Turn Gently*, Island Press, 1979; *A Dandelion for Van Gogh*, Angus&Robertson, 1985; *The Life On Water and the Life Beneath*, Penguin Books Australia, 1995; *Selected Poems*, Penguin Books Australia, 1995; and *Public Private*, Vagabond Press, 2013. We are grateful to Michael Brennan of Vagabond Press for permission to reprint all the poems in that collection.

With thanks to Rob Shield for his care with the poems, particularly in the 'Return to Baghdad' section of the manuscript.

About the author

J.S. Harry published eight books of poetry in her lifetime, including *The Deer Under The Skin* (1971), one of the first titles in the historic UQP Paperback Poets series; *Hold, for a little while, and turn gently* (1979); *A Dandelion for Van Gogh* (1985), which was shortlisted for the National Book Council and the Adelaide Festival Poetry Awards; *The Life on Water and the Life Beneath* (1995); *Selected Poems* (1995), winner of the NSW Premier's Award for Poetry; *Sun Shadow, Moon Shadow* (2000); and *Public Private* (2013). Her collection of Peter Henry Lepus poems, *Not Finding Wittgenstein* (published by Giramondo in 2007) won the *Age* Poetry Book of the Year Award.

Nicolette Stasko is the author of six collections of poetry, *Abundance, Black Night with Windows, Dwelling in the Shape of Things, In Certain Light, The Weight of Irises* and *Glass Cathedrals: New and Selected Poems.*